MASTIFF SECRETS:

The Ultimate Guide

Everything You Need to Know About Buying, Raising, and Caring for a Mastiff

Mastiff Secrets

CHAPTER 1	9
ORIGIN AND HISTORY	**9**
MASTIFFS AS WAR DOGS	9
MASTIFFS IN BRITAIN	10
MASTIFFS IN THE UNITED STATES	10
FROM WAR DOGS TO GENTLE PETS	11

CHAPTER 2	12
APPEARANCE AND BREED STANDARD	**12**
SIZE	12
COLORING AND COAT	12
OTHER PHYSICAL CHARACTERISTICS	13
BREED STANDARDS	13
American Style	*13*
Old English Style	*16*

CHAPTER 3	19
GENTLE GIANT: THE MASTIFF'S TEMPERAMENT	**19**
GENERAL TEMPERAMENT	19
CHILDREN	20
FAMILY	20
STRANGERS	20
OTHER DOGS	21
OTHER ANIMALS	22

CHAPTER 4	23
BUYING A MASTIFF	**23**
WHY YOU SHOULD GET A MASTIFF	23
ON THE OTHER HAND…	23
ASKING THE RIGHT QUESTIONS	24
Why do you want a Mastiff?	*24*
Do you want a puppy or an adult dog?	*24*
How much are you willing to spend?	*25*
How do you choose a breeder?	*25*
How do you choose a puppy?	*26*
THE CONTRACT	26
WHAT ABOUT RESCUE GROUPS?	32
WHAT ABOUT PET SHOPS?	32

CHAPTER 5 — 33

PUPPY LOVE: BRINGING HOME YOUR MASTIFF PUPPY — 33

- GO SHOPPING — 33
- PUPPY-PROOF YOUR HOUSE — 34
- PREPARE A PLACE FOR THE NEW PUPPY — 35
- TEACH THE HOUSE RULES — 35
- BE AVAILABLE — 35
- BE GENTLE — 36
- SCHEDULE AN APPOINTMENT WITH YOUR VET — 36
- FEEDING YOUR MASTIFF PUPPY. — 36
- THE FIRST DAY AND NIGHT IN A NEW HOME — 37

CHAPTER 6 — 38

DIET AND GROOMING TIPS — 38

- DIET — 38
  - *The puppy years* — 38
  - *Adult dogs* — 39
  - *What food to choose* — 39
  - *How much food?* — 39
  - *A grown-up bowl* — 39
  - *Water* — 40
  - *Bones* — 40
- GROOMING — 41
  - *Starting early* — 41
  - *Bathing* — 41
  - *Brushing* — 42
  - *Cleaning ears* — 42
  - *Cleaning eyes* — 42
  - *Clipping toenails* — 43
  - *Other grooming* — 43

CHAPTER 7 — 44

KEEPING YOUR MASTIFF HEALTHY — 44

- EXERCISE — 44
- PLAYTIME — 44
- COMMON HEALTH PROBLEMS — 45
  - *Progressive Retinal Atrophy* — 45
  - *Hip Dysplasia* — 46
  - *Hypothyroidism* — 46
  - *Osteochrondritis Dissecans (OCD)* — 46

Arthritis — 46
Bloat — 47
Elbow and knee bursas — 47
Cruciate Knee Rupture — 47

CHAPTER 8 — 48
FIRST AID FOR YOUR MASTIFF — 48

CHOOSE A VET — 48
KEEP GOOD RECORDS — 48
EVALUATING YOUR MASTIFF'S CONDITION — 49
Capillary refill time — 49
Respiration — 49
Pulse — 49
Temperature — 49
Hydration — 49
DEALING WITH EMERGENCIES — 50
Shock — 50
Bloat — 50
Overeating — 51
Gastric Dilation/Volvulus — 51
External bleeding — 52
Internal bleeding — 52
Choking — 53
Foreign body in the mouth or esophagus — 53
Convulsions — 54
Ear injuries — 54
Eye injuries — 55
Electrical shock — 55
Allergic reactions — 55
Frostbite — 56
Hit by a car — 56

CHAPTER 9 — 57
SOCIALIZING AND TRAINING THE MASTIFF — 57

SOCIALIZATION — 57
OBEDIENCE TRAINING — 58
BASIC COMMANDS — 59
Sit — 59
Down — 60
Stay — 60
Come — 60
Leash training — 61
HOUSETRAINING — 61

CHAPTER 10   63

BREEDING YOUR MASTIFF   63

Are you ready for breeding?   63
Is your female ready for breeding?   64
Choosing a breeding partner   64
The breeding environment   65
Caring for the pregnant female   65
Time for puppies   65
When to call the vet   67

CHAPTER 11   68

CARING FOR YOUR MASTIFF AS IT AGES   68

Nutrition   68
Supplements   69
What your veterinarian should check   69
    Cardiac disease   69
    Renal disease   70
    Gum inflammation and dental disease   71
    Adult-onset megaesophagus   71
    Tumors of the spleen   72
    Spinal cord problems   72
    Incompetent sphincters   72
    Prostate problems   72
    Arthritis   73

CHAPTER 12   74

RESOURCES AND FAQS   74

Resources   74
FAQs   75
    Where should I get a Mastiff?   75
    What if I don't want a puppy?   75
    What about a pet shop?   75
    What about a backyard breeder?   75
    Should my Mastiff live indoors or out?   76
    What kind of living quarters does a Mastiff require? Where do they sleep?   76
    What other stuff do I need to buy for my Mastiff?   76
    What are Mastiffs like in the house?   78
    How much slobber are we talking about?   78
    And how much do Mastiffs shed?   78
    Do Mastiffs chew?   78
    Do Mastiffs bark much?   78
    Do Mastiffs bite?   79

Do Mastiffs pass gas?   *79*
Do Mastiffs roam?   *79*
Do Mastiffs smell?   *79*
Do Mastiffs snore?   *79*
How much does a Mastiff cost?   *79*
Does owning a Mastiff cost a lot?   *80*
What does a Mastiff eat?   *80*
How much does a Mastiff eat?   *80*
How much does a Mastiff weigh?   *80*
Do Mastiffs need a lot of exercise?   *80*
Do Mastiffs get along with children?   *81*
Do Mastiffs get along with other dogs?   *81*
Do Mastiffs get along with other animals?   *81*
Do Mastiffs get along with strangers?   *81*
Do Mastiffs make good guard dogs?   *81*
How much training does a Mastiff need?   *82*
Do Mastiffs make good obedience dogs?   *82*
What colors are Mastiffs?   *82*
How long does a Mastiff live?   *83*
What health problems do Mastiffs tend to have?   *83*
What kind of a temperament does a Mastiff have?   *83*
How much grooming does a Mastiff need?   *83*
Are there any famous book and movie Mastiffs?   *84*
What's the difference between a Mastiff and a Bullmastiff?   *84*

FOREWORD

"What the Lion is to the Cat
the Mastiff is to the Dog,
the noblest of the family;
he stands alone,
and all others sink before him.
His courage does not exceed
his temper and generosity,
and in attachment he equals
the kindest of his race."

Cynographia Britannica – 1800

If you have ever owned a Mastiff, you have heard all the questions and comments:

- Is that a dog or a pony?
- How much does he eat?
- How much does she weigh?
- That is the biggest dog I have ever seen!

And chances are, the Mastiff really is the biggest dog the observer has ever seen! With full-grown male Mastiffs weighing from 170 to 220 pounds and at least 30 inches tall at the shoulder, mastiffs are the largest dogs around. Great Danes and Irish Wolfhounds may be taller, but they are lightweights compared with the Mastiff.

Mastiffs are also called English mastiffs or Old English Mastiffs. They may be large, but they are truly gentle giants. If they are well socialized as puppies, they grow up to be gentle, patient, and affectionate dogs that are good with children, good with other dogs, and intensely loyal to their families. Consequently, they make wonderful pets, companions, and watchdogs.

If you own a Mastiff or are considering getting one, this book will answer your questions about how to choose and raise your puppy and how to care for your dog. Read on to learn more about this wonderful dog breed!

Chapter 1
ORIGIN AND HISTORY

Mastiffs in one form or another have been around since before recorded history began. Carvings from the Babylonian palace of Ashurbanipal (now on display in the British Museum) show Mastiff-type dogs hunting lions in the desert near the Tigris River.

Mastiffs as war dogs

Phoenician traders introduced the Mastiff to ancient Britain in the 6th century BC. The ancient Celts began using them as war dogs who accompanied their masters into battle. This was the beginning of a long history of Mastiffs as fighters, soldiers, protectors, and watchdogs. A popular story tells that when Sir Peers Legh was wounded in the Battle of Agincourt, his Mastiff stood over him and protected him for many hours throughout the battle.

When the Romans invaded Britain, they took Mastiffs back to Italy and used them to guard property and prisoners, as well as to fight in the arena. The Mastiff is reported to have been Julius Caesar's favorite dog. Kubla Khan kept a kennel of 5,000 Mastiffs for hunting and war. When Hannibal crossed the Alps, he took several battalions of war Mastiffs.

Mastiffs in Britain

Back in Britain, the Mastiff was one of the few breeds mentioned by name in The Forest Laws of King Canute, the first written laws of England. Mastiffs were mentioned as being kept for protection, and the middle toes of their front feet had to be removed so the dogs could not run fast enough to catch deer (which traditionally belonged to royalty).
British royals kept Mastiffs to guard their castles and estates, releasing them at night to ward off intruders. Henry VIII is said to have presented Charles V of Spain with 400 Mastiffs to be used in battle.

From the 12th through 19th centuries, Mastiffs were used for bear-baiting. This "sport," in which dogs attacked chained-up bears, bulls, and even tigers, was especially popular during Queen Elizabeth's time. Such fights were often staged for the queen's entertainment.
The size of the Mastiff and its need to eat about as much food per day as an adult man made a Mastiff too costly for most common folk, except butchers, who had enough meat scraps to feed a Mastiff well. Therefore, the Mastiff was often called the "Butcher's Dog."

Mastiffs in the United States

The first Mastiff in the "new world" was brought from Britain on the Mayflower by the Pilgrims. The breed didn't become popular in America until the 1800s, when Mastiffs were frequently found on plantations in the South as property guards.

During the World Wars, Mastiffs were used to pull munitions carts at the front lines. However, their popularity was declining at the same time, partly because of their size: It was considered unpatriotic to keep a dog that ate as much in one day as a soldier. By the 1920s, Mastiffs were almost extinct in Britain, and by the end of World War II, Canada and the United States were sending Mastiffs to Britain to save the breed. Now, the breed is well-established in both continents.

From war dogs to gentle pets

How did Mastiffs change from hunting and war dogs to the gentle pets we know today? Part of the reason is that breeders have bred the Mastiff for gentleness and have thus created an excellent companion. In addition, Mastiffs are simply treated differently today. No longer are they sent into battle or baited against bears. Instead, Mastiffs are either kept as pets or put to use as watchdogs, guards, police or military dogs, search and rescue dogs, or as weight pullers.

Chapter 2
APPEARANCE AND BREED STANDARD

The general term "mastiff" refers to many different breeds around the world, probably all descended from the same root stock. These include such breeds as the Bull Mastiff, Neapolitan Mastiff, and Tibetan Mastiff. All the large mountain dogs of Spain, France, Turkey, and the Balkans can be traced to Mastiff blood in their ancestry. Even the Chow Chow carries Mastiff blood, as does the Pug, which was originally a form of dwarf Mastiff.

The Mastiff breed itself, however, refers to the specific breed that originated in England more than 2,000 years ago. This chapter deals with the Mastiff breed's appearance and breed standards.

Size

Mastiffs are massive, powerful, and muscular. The males are upward of 30 inches high and weigh 180 to 220 pounds, and the females are 27 inches and about 150 pounds. The Guinness Book of World Records says the largest dog in the world was Zorba, a Mastiff from the United Kingdom. Zorba weighed 343 pounds and measured almost 8 feet from nose to tail!

Coloring and Coat

Mastiffs have a medium to short coat that is golden fawn, light fawn, apricot, silver, or brindle in color. Regardless of their overall coloring, they have a black mask and ears and very little white fur.

Mastiff Secrets

Other physical characteristics

Mastiffs have a heavy square head with a short muzzle. Their eyes are small, dark, and hazel. The teeth should meet in a scissors or slightly undershot bite. The tail is set quite high, tapers to the tip, and reaches to the hocks.

Breed standards

There are actually two breed standards for a Mastiff: the "American Style" as defined by the American Kennel Association, and the "Old English Style" as defined by the UK Kennel Club.

American Style

Below is the AKC Official Breed Standard for the American Style Mastiff.

General Appearance	The mastiff is a large, massive, symmetrical dog with a well-knit frame. The impression is one of grandeur and dignity. Dogs are more massive throughout. Bitches should not be faulted for being somewhat smaller in all dimensions while maintaining a proportionally powerful structure. A good evaluation considers positive qualities of type and soundness with equal weight.
Size	<ul><li>Dogs: minimum 30 inches at the shoulder.</li><li>Bitches: minimum 27.5 inches at the shoulder.</li><li>Fault: Dogs or bitches below the minimum standard. The farther below the standard, the greater the fault.</li></ul>
Proportion	Rectangular, the length of the dog from fore chest to rump is somewhat longer than the height at the withers. The height of the dog should come from depth of body rather than from length of legs.
Substance	<ul><li>Massive, heavy boned, with a powerful muscle structure. Great depth and breadth desirable.</li><li>Fault: Lack of substance or slab sided.</li></ul>
Head	In general, outline giving a massive appearance when viewed from any angle. Breadth greatly desired.
Eyes	<ul><li>Set wide apart, medium in size, never too prominent.</li><li>Expression alert but kindly.</li><li>Color of eyes brown, the darker the better, and showing no haw. Light eyes or a predatory expression is undesirable.</li></ul>
Ears	<ul><li>Small in proportion to the skull</li><li>V-shaped, rounded at the tips</li><li>Leather moderately thin, set widely apart at the highest points on the sides of the skull continuing the outline</li></ul>

	across the summit. • Lie close to the cheeks when in repose. • Dark in color, the blacker the better, conforming to the color of the muzzle.
Skull	• Broad and somewhat flattened between the ears • Forehead slightly curved, showing marked wrinkles that are particularly distinctive when at attention. • Brows (superciliary ridges) moderately raised. • Muscles of the temples well developed, those of the cheeks extremely powerful. • Arch across the skull a flattened curve with a furrow up the center of the forehead. This extends from between the eyes to halfway up the skull.
Stop	• Well marked but not too abrupt. • Muzzle should be half the length of the skull, thus dividing the head into three parts - one for the foreface and two for the skull. In other words, the distance from the tip of the nose to the stop is equal to one-half the length of the occiput. • Circumference of the muzzle (measured midway between the eyes and nose) to that of the head (measured before the ears) is as 3 is to 5.
Muzzle	• Short, broad under the eyes and running nearly equal in width to the end of nose. • Truncated, i.e. blunt and cut off square, thus forming a right angle with the upper line of the face. • Of great depth from the point of nose to the underjaw. • Underjaw broad to the end and slightly rounded. • Muzzle dark, the blacker the better. • Fault: Snipiness of the muzzle.
Nose	Broad and always dark, the blacker the better, with spread flat nostrils (not pointed or turned up) in profile.
Lips	Diverging at obtuse angles with the septum and sufficiently pendulous so as to show a modified square profile.
Canine Teeth	• Healthy and wide apart. • Jaws powerful. • Scissors bite preferred, but a moderately undershot jaw should not be faulted providing the teeth are not visible when the mouth is closed.
Neck	• Powerful, very muscular, slightly arched, and of medium length. • Gradually increases in circumference as it approaches the shoulder. • Neck moderately "dry" (not showing an excess of loose skin).

Topline	In profile the topline should be straight, level, and firm, not too swaybacked, roached, or dropping off sharply behind the high point of the rump.
Chest	<ul><li>Wide, deep, rounded, and well let down between the forelegs, extending at least to the elbow.</li><li>Fore chest should be deep and well defined with the breastbone extending in front of the foremost point of the shoulders.</li><li>Ribs well rounded.</li><li>False ribs deep and well set back.</li></ul>
Underline	There should be a reasonable, but not exaggerated, tuck-up.
Back	<ul><li>Muscular, powerful, and straight.</li><li>When viewed from the rear, there should be a slight rounding over the rump.</li></ul>
Loins	Wide and muscular.
Tail	<ul><li>Set on moderately high and reaching to the hocks or a little below.</li><li>Wide at the root, tapering to the end, hanging straight in repose, forming a slight curve, but never over the back when the dog is in motion.</li></ul>
Shoulders	<ul><li>Moderately sloping, powerful and muscular, with no tendency to looseness.</li><li>Degree of front angulation to match correct rear angulation.</li></ul>
Legs	Straight, strong and set wide apart, heavy boned.
Elbows	Parallel to body.
Pasterns	Strong and bent only slightly.
Feet	<ul><li>Large, round, and compact with well-arched toes.</li><li>Black nails preferred</li></ul>
Hindquarters	Broad, wide and muscular.
Second thighs	Well developed, leading to a strong hock joint.
Stifle joint	Moderately angulated matching the front
Rear legs	<ul><li>Wide apart and parallel when viewed from the rear.</li><li>When the portion of the leg below the hock is correctly "set back" and perpendicular to the ground, a plumb line dropped from the rearmost point of the hindquarters will pass in front of the foot. This rules out straight hocks, and because stifle angulation varies with hock angulation, it also rules out insufficiently angulated stifles.</li><li>Fault: Straight stifles.</li></ul>

Coat	Outer coat straight, coarse and moderately short. Undercoat dense, short, and close lying. Coat should not be as long as to produce "fringe" on the belly, tail, or hind legs. Fault: Long or wavy coat.
Color	- Fawn, apricot, or brindle. Brindle should have fawn or apricot as a background color, which should be completely covered with very dark stripes.
- Muzzle, ears, and nose must be dark, the blacker the better, with similar color tone around the eye orbits and extending upward between them.
- A small patch of white on the chest is permitted.
- Faults: Excessive white on the chest or white on any other part of the body. Mask, ears, or nose lacking dark pigment.
Gait	- The gait denotes power and strength.
- The rear legs should have drive, while the forelegs should track smoothly with good reach.
- In motion, the legs move straight forward; as the dog's speed increases from a walk to a trot, the feet move in under the center line of the body to maintain balance.
Temperament	- A combination of grandeur and good nature, courage and docility.
- Dignity, rather than gaiety, is the mastiff's correct demeanor. Judges should condone shyness or viciousness.
- Conversely, judges should also beware of putting a premium on showiness.

Old English Style

Below is the Kennel Club Official Breed Standard for the Old English Style Mastiff.

| General Appearance | - Head, in general outline, giving a square appearance when viewed from any point.
- Breadth greatly desired: in ratio to length of whole head and face as 2/3.
- Body massive, broad, deep, long, powerfully built, on legs wide apart and squarely set.
- Muscles sharply defined.
- Size a great desideratum, if combined with quality.
- Height and substance important if both points are proportionately combined. |
|---|---|
| Characteristics | - Large, massive, powerful, symmetrical, and well-knit frame.
- A combination of grandeur and courage. |

Temperament	- Calm. - Affectionate to owners. - Capable of guarding.
Head and Skull	- Skull broad between ears, forehead flat, but wrinkled when attention is excited. - Brows (superciliary ridges) slightly raised. - Muscles of temples and cheeks (temporal and masseter) well developed. - Arch across skull of a rounded, flattened curve, with a depression up center of forehead from median line between eyes, to half way up sagittal suture. - Face or muzzle, short, broad under eyes and keeping nearly parallel in width to end of nose; Truncated, i.e., blunt and cut off squarely, thus forming a right angle with upper line of face, of great depth from point of nose to underjaw. - Underjaw broad to end. - Nose broad, with widely spreading nostrils when viewed from front, flat (not pointed or turned up) in profile. - Lips diverging at obtuse angles with septum, and slightly pendulous so as to show a square profile. - Length of muzzle to whole head and face as 1/3. - Circumference of muzzle (measured midway between eyes and nose) to that of head (measured before the ears) as 3/5.
Eyes	- Small, wide apart, divided by at least space of two eyes. - Stop between eyes well marked but not too abrupt. - Colored hazel brown, darker the better, showing no haw.
Ears	- Small. - Thin to touch. - Wide apart. - Set on at highest points of sides of skull, so as to continue outline across summit. - Laying flat and close to cheeks when in repose.
Mouth	- Canine teeth healthy, powerful and wide apart. - Incisors level, or lower projecting beyond upper but never so much as to become visible when mouth is closed.
Neck	- Slightly arched. - Moderately long. - Very muscular. - Measuring in circumference about one or two inches less than skull before ears.

Forequarters	- Shoulder and arm slightly sloping, heavy, and muscular. - Legs straight, strong, and set wide apart; bones being large. - Elbows square. - Pasterns upright.
Body	- Chest wide, deep, and well let down between forelegs. - Ribs arched and well rounded. - False ribs deep and well set back to hips. - Girth one-third more than height at shoulder. - Back and loins wide and muscular; flat and very wide In bitch slightly arched in a dog. - Great depth of flanks.
Hindquarters	- Broad, wide and muscular. - Well-developed second thighs. - Hocks bent, wide apart, and quite squarely set when standing or walking.
Feet	- Large and round. - Toes well arched. - Nails black.
Tail	- Set on high, and reaching to hocks, or a little below them. - Wide at its root and tapering to end. - Hanging straight in repose, but forming a curve with end pointing upwards, but not over back, when dog is excited.
Gait/Movement	Powerful, easy extension.
Coat	Short and close lying, but not too fine over shoulders, neck and back.
Color	- Apricot-fawn, silver-fawn, fawn, or dark fawn-brindle. - Muzzle ears and nose should be black with black around the orbits, and extending upward between them.
Faults	Any departure from the foregoing points should be considered a fault and the seriousness with which the fault should be regarded is in exact proportion to its degree. Note: Males should have two apparently normal testicles fully descended into the scrotum.

Chapter 3
GENTLE GIANT:
THE MASTIFF'S TEMPERAMENT

Former warrior dogs. Used to fight lions, tigers, and bears. Still the largest dog in the world. Obviously not a quiet and friendly family dog, right? Absolutely wrong! Yes, it is true the Mastiff was a great warrior in the past. But today's Mastiff is gentle, patient, and affectionate. If you have any concerns about how your Mastiff will relate to children, family members, strangers, other dogs, and other animals, then this chapter will put your fears at rest.

General temperament

Mastiffs, like people, are highly individual. Most are calm and placid, but some are full of energy and need to be kept busy. A lot of any Mastiff's behavior depends on how well it was socialized while young.

Mastiffs have a somewhat contradictory nature. They are very sensitive and can be crushed by harsh words. They are also eager to please. On the other hand, Mastiffs tend to be stubborn. It can be very challenging to get a Mastiff to do something it doesn't want to do.

Because Mastiffs are so big, many people think they are stupid, slow, and clumsy. This is far from the truth. Yes, Mastiffs do tend to drool and wheeze a lot and to snore loudly. However, they are intelligent and dignified dogs who learn quickly and are eager to please.

As for Mastiffs being slow, they are actually quite fast and can outrun any human being. Of course, they also would rather stay with their family than do anything else, so they typically won't run away if let loose. All told, the Mastiff is an ideal family dog for anyone who wants a big, loyal friend and who can tolerate the snoring and drooling.

Children

The Mastiff is typically calm and gentle, and is therefore an excellent companion for children, especially older children. It is perhaps not the best choice for toddlers, simply because of its sheer size.

If you have young children, the ideal situation is to get a Mastiff puppy and raise it along with the children. Chances are, you will have to teach your children to be dog-friendly more than you will have to teach the dog to be child-friendly!

If you have a Mastiff and then a child joins your family, you will likely find that you have a loyal and protective "babysitter." Even an adult dog that isn't used to children at all will quickly learn to deal with them.

Family

The Mastiff is a great family dog — relaxed, calm, and peaceful. You will have to make concessions for its size, such as buying a bigger car than you might otherwise choose. You'll be surprised, though, to learn that you don't need a huge house with acres of land. The Mastiff tends to be lazy, and it will live quite happily in an apartment, as long as it is close to you.

The Mastiff is a social breed and needs lots of companionship. It loves to spend time with its family and is very affectionate. It will be happiest when it gets to spend the entire day — and night — close to you. So plan to spend a lot of time together, taking walks, playing fetch, or just sitting together and enjoying a book or movie. The Mastiff is definitely not a dog to pen in the back yard and only visit occasionally or to leave alone day and night while everyone else goes to work and school.

Strangers

The world is full of people who are strangers to you and your dog. When it comes to strangers, Mastiffs are much like people: some are extroverted and friendly, loving to meet new people, while others are more introverted and aloof. Mastiffs tend overall to be shy, but a properly socialized Mastiff will stand or sit beside you politely when a stranger is around. It will wait to take its cues from you as to whether the stranger is a new friend. It may take some time for your Mastiff to accept new people into the "pack," but once a new person has visited your home a few times, your Mastiff will accept them as friends.

Although Mastiffs are gentle, they are also brave and loyal watchdogs. They don't need training to be guards because they simply assume that is their job. Mastiffs rarely bark, but they are naturally protective of their territory and home. A Mastiff won't attack strangers and intruders; instead, it will hold them at bay until directed otherwise. If someone comes too close without permission, even the friendliest Mastiff might grab an arm as a warning, but typically it will not bite.

Other dogs

If a Mastiff is well socialized as a puppy, then it will get along well with other dogs as an adult. See Chapter 9, *Training the Mastiff*, for tips on how to ensure that your Mastiff behaves well in this area.

Assuming that your Mastiff was well socialized, it should be as calm and patient with other dogs as it is with children. In fact, most Mastiffs love playing with small dogs. The Mastiff is peaceful and tolerant, and usually will just turn its back even if attacked. It will not fight unless it has to in order to protect itself or a member of the family.

If your Mastiff was unfortunately not well socialized as a puppy, then it may be aggressive toward other dogs. In this case, it is best not to place such a dog in the same family as another dog of the same sex. When your puppy matures, the two dogs will fight for dominance.

If you are concerned that your Mastiff is overly aggressive, you have several avenues to try:

- Consult a professional trainer to see whether your dog can be retrained
- Have your veterinarian check for physical problems that can affect behavior, especially hormone problems such as hypothyroidism
- Consider having your dog spayed or neutered, which will reduce its tendencies to fight or dominate another dog
- Change to a food that is lower in protein — no more than 18% protein

If your Mastiff does get into a fight, do NOT get between the fighting dogs. People known to the dogs should grab each dog by the rear legs and drag them away from each other. Do not let them see each other or the fight may start again.

Other animals

Although the Mastiffs' ancestors may have been hunters, the modern-day Mastiff lives peaceably with other animals. This isn't to say that your Mastiff won't chase a rabbit, squirrel, or cat if given the chance. However, it will quickly learn the difference between a squirrel in the back yard and a fellow pet in its own household or even the neighbor's garden.

A Mastiff's reaction to other animals depends largely on how well socialized the Mastiff was as a puppy. Also, Mastiffs vary individually in their reactions to other animals — some may love to chase cats; others tolerate or ignore them. A Mastiff who grows up around other animals, whether a cat in an apartment or a chicken on a farm, will likely get along well with all other animals.

Chapter 4
BUYING A MASTIFF

If you are considering buying a Mastiff, this chapter will help you weigh the pros and cons of your decision and then help you choose the best animal for your needs.

Why you should get a Mastiff

Thinking about getting a Mastiff? There are many good reasons, among them that Mastiffs are --

- Affectionate, gentle, loyal, and intelligent
- Calm and quiet, barking very little
- Patient with children
- Not aggressive with other dogs (it generally will not fight even if provoked)
- Natural protectors that make great watchdogs
- Not interested in hunting or running away
- Eager to please

On the other hand...

Before you make your final decision, consider these negative aspects of owning a Mastiff. Make sure you can handle these negatives before you bring a Mastiff into your home and heart:

- They are big and heavy
- Although not very active, they do take up a lot of space
- They eat a lot

- They drool, snore, wheeze, pass gas, and have bad breath
- They don't have a long lifespan (8-12 years)
- They are expensive: "pet quality" animals cost $600-$800 and "show-quality" animals cost up to $3000
- Considering the costs of food, medicine, and other necessary items, they are expensive to maintain

If you do decide to get a Mastiff, be prepared for lots of attention whenever you leave your house together. People will stop to ask questions, usually about how much your dog weighs and how much it eats.

Asking the right questions

If you have decided to get a Mastiff, you now have some decisions to make:

Why do you want a Mastiff?

Mastiffs are excellent pets, companions, and friends. They are loyal and affectionate. If you are looking for a family dog, a Mastiff is an excellent choice.

Mastiffs can also be trained as "working dogs." They can be therapy workers, watchdogs, and search-and-rescue dogs.

And finally, Mastiffs can be show dogs. With the proper training and conditioning, they can excel at carting, tracking, obedience, conformation showing, and weight pulling.

So why do you want a Mastiff? Your needs will be different depending on whether you want a companion, a co-worker, or a show dog.

Do you want a puppy or an adult dog?

Whether to buy a puppy or an adult dog depends a great deal on how much time and energy you want to put into training. If you don't want to deal with house-breaking and training your dog, then you obviously do not want a puppy. You will want an older dog.

On the other hand, if you buy an adult dog, you often don't know how the dog was raised, how healthy it is, or how good its bloodlines are. Was the dog properly socialized as a puppy so it now reacts well to other dogs? Was the dog trained with love and affection or anger and hitting? If knowing these things is important to you, then you should look for a puppy and be prepared to put the necessary time and energy into socializing it.

How much are you willing to spend?

Mastiffs are expensive, especially if you want a show dog. Prices are normally higher if the parents are healthy and have achieved good results in dog shows. In addition, the purchase price may vary depending on whether you are buying a pet or a show dog. A pet will be less expensive and will come with a no-breeding clause.

In addition to your initial purchase price, Mastiffs are expensive to live with. Their food costs more, their medicine costs more, they need bigger crates and beds — you might even need to buy a bigger car so everyone has somewhere to sit. Are you prepared to spend the money not only to purchase your Mastiff, but also to support it and keep it healthy?

How do you choose a breeder?

If you go to Google and type "English Mastiff Breeders," you will receive back almost 13,000 entries. How can you possibly select a reputable breeder?

First of all, take your time. You are buying a dog that will be your companion and friend for the next decade. Take time to do research so you do finally choose a good breeder. How will you know when you have found a good breeder? A good breeder will —

- Breed only Mastiffs that are show champions, quality animals that are typical of their breed in both appearance and temperament
- Have experience and not just be breeding a pet in the back yard to make extra money
- Plan carefully which male and which female dog to mate, in order to pass positive qualities on to the next generation
- Have documentation from a veterinarian showing the parents are generally healthy and free from the most common diseases
- Allow you to meet the puppy's parents
- Take care of the puppies, allowing them to stay full time with the mother for the first few weeks of life, providing quality food once they begin eating, and making sure they receive their initial shots
- Not release the puppies from their mother until they are at least seven weeks old
- Register the puppies with the American Kennel Club (in the United States), the UK Kennel Club (in Great Britain), or another reputable dog club
- Offer a written contract

To find a reputable breeder, do your homework. Visit dog shows, read books and magazines, ask questions, and get recommendations.

How do you choose a puppy?

Once you have chosen a breeder, it is time to choose a puppy. You should choose a puppy whose temperament fits well into your family.

Puppy personality

Even puppies in the same litter have different personalities. One of the most important personality aspects to consider is whether a submissive or dominant dog will fit better in your family.

Do you have small children, elderly people, or another dog already living in your house? If so, you should choose a puppy that seems calm and subordinate. This doesn't necessarily mean the dog is shy or timid, just that it won't try to dominate the house, challenge your authority, or compete with another dog.

Also note that if you already have another dog, you should choose a puppy of the opposite sex.

On the other hand, if you are experienced with large dogs and plan to take the time to train this puppy, you could choose a puppy with more dominant tendencies. Dominant should not mean aggressive, but this dog will be more challenging to raise.

The parents

When you meet your puppy's parents, examine their personalities. After all, your puppy will inherit at least some personality traits from its sire and dam.

Following are some things to note:

- How does the mother respond to you when you meet her the first time? Is she nervous or calm? Is she excited or shy? Is she friendly or aggressive?
- Does the mother let you pet her without any problems?
- Does the mother let you touch her puppies without any problems?
- Do both parents look healthy?

The contract

A breeder contract ensures that the breeder is willing to stand behind the dog and guarantees that you will receive a quality animal. Of course, no matter how healthy the bloodline and how extensive the genetic testing, no one can guarantee a 100% healthy dog. Too many factors influence the health of your dog, including the quality of care it receives in your home.

Examine your breeder contract in detail. What is the breeder's policy if there is a problem with your Mastiff? Does the breeder offer a replacement guarantee? If so, do you have to first send back the dog you already have (and have probably grown attached to)? The best contract guarantees you a new puppy for free or at a discounted rate, while allowing you to keep the dog you already have.

If you are getting a puppy as a pet, the contract will typically include a "no-breeding" clause. This ensures that the Mastiff breed improves because only the best examples are used for breeding.

The following pages show a sample contract.

Mastiff Secrets

MASTIFF PUPPY CONTRACT

FOR THIS CONTRACT SELLER SHALL BE _____ , THIS AGREEMENT WAS MADE ON DATE. _____

BETWEEN_____ AND BUYER.

NAME _____
ADDRESS_____
PHONE NUMBER _____
EMAIL _____

THE SELLER AGREES TO SELL ONE REGISTERED MASTIFF PUP
SEX M F
WHELPED, DAY____ MONTH_____YEAR___
TATTOO # _____
PUP SOLD OPEN TO BREED NO_ YES
SALES PRICE _____
DEPOSIT PAID _____
AMOUNT DUE _____
DATE PAID IN FULL_____
CHECK CASH
DEPOSIT NON REFUNDABLE.

THE SELLER GUARANTEES
- THE PUP IN GOOD HEALTH AT THE TIME OF SALE.
- THE PUP WILL BE WORMED AND HAVE ITS FIRST SET OF VACCINATIONS.
- THE PUP WILL BE VET-CHECKED HEALTHY BEFORE LEAVING.
- THE PUP WILL BE FREE OF HIP DYSPLASIA FOR 2 YEARS FROM DATE OF PURCHASE.
- THE PUP WILL BE FREE OF ANY LIFE-THREATENING "GENETIC" HEALTH CONDITIONS OF THE HEART AND LUNGS AND DIGESTIVE SYSTEMS FOR 2 YEARS FROM DATE OF PURCHASE

OTHER HEALTH PROBLEM THE DOG MAY EXPERIENCE WILL BE REVIEWED BY THE SELLER AND HIS VETERINARIAN AND IT WILL BE AT THE DISCRETION OF THE SELLER AS TO WHETHER THERE ARE

GROUNDS FOR COMPENSATION. THE BUYER AGREES TO ACCEPT THE DECISION OF THE SELLER IN SUCH CIRCUMSTANCES.

THE BUYER AGREES THAT MALADIES COMMON TO LARGE BREEDS, SUCH AS BLOAT AND CRUCIATES, ARE CONDITIONS THAT WILL NOT BE COVERED UNDER THIS CONTRACT. THE BUYER AGREES TO NOT SEEK COMPENSATION FOR THESE CONDITIONS.

BECAUSE ENTROPIA IS OFTEN ATTRIBUTABLE TO HEAVY "TYPE" AND DEEP WRINKLES, ENTROPIA IS EXCLUDED FROM COMPENSATION UNDER THIS CONTRACT, AND BUYER AGREES TO SEEK NO COMPENSATION FOR THIS CONDITION.

THE BUYER AGREES THAT THERE SHALL BE NO HEALTH GUARANTEE AFTER 2 YEARS FROM DATE OF PURCHASE.

SELLER WILL EITHER PAY VET COSTS PERTAINING TO GENETIC MEDICAL CONDITIONS COVERED UNDER THIS CONTRACT TO A LIMIT OF $600.00 OR SELLER MAY CHOOSE TO TAKE THE PUP BACK AND REPLACE IT WITH A HEALTHY PUP FROM THE NEXT AVAILABLE LITTER. BREEDER WILL NOT BOTH REPLACE PUP AND COVER VET COST. THESE OPTIONS ARE BREEDER'S CHOICE.

BUYER AGREES TO HAVE THE PUP CHECKED BY THEIR VET WITHIN FIVE DAYS OF RECEIVING THE PUP.

BUYER MUST NOTIFY SELLER IMMEDIATELY OF ANY HEALTH CONCERNS COVERED UNDER THIS CONTRACT.

BUYER AGREES TO GIVE SELLER FULL ACCESS TO THE PUP'S FULL MEDICAL RECORDS IN THE EVENT THE PUP HAS A HEALTH PROBLEM COVERED UNDER THIS CONTRACT.

SELLER HAS THE RIGHT BEFORE PAYING VET BILLS OR REPLACING PUP TO HAVE THE PUP CHECKED BY A VET OF SELLER'S CHOICE.

BUYER WILL KEEP PUP IN GOOD HEALTH, AND WILL FEED IT ONLY FOOD RECOMMENDED BY BREEDER. IAMS, NUTRO, CANADIAN, HAPPY PAWS, NATURES RECIPES, KASCO, SOLID GOLD, SCIENCE DIET, EUKANUBA, OR RAW AND HOME-COOKED FOODS. OR OTHER FOODS APPROVED BY BREEDER.

BUYER AGREES TO KEEP PUP UP-TO-DATE ON ALL VACCINATIONS AND WORMING.

BUYER SWEARS THIS PUP WILL NOT BE USED FOR EXPERIMENTATION OR TO BE SOLD IN AUCTION OR TO A DOG BROKER OR TO BE RESOLD IN A PET STORE. IF THIS PUP IS USED FOR ANY OF THE ABOVE PURPOSES, BUYER GIVES THE SELLER THE RIGHT TO ENTER ANY PROPERTY THE PUP IS ON TO REPOSESS THE PUP ON THE GROUNDS THAT THE DOG WAS BOUGHT UNDER FALSE PRETENSES. BUYER AGREES NOT TO SUE SELLER SHOULD SELLER HAVE TO REPOSESS PUP THAT WAS SOLD IN PET STORE, SOLD AT AUCTION, USED FOR EXPERIMENTATION, OR SHIPPED OR SOLD TO A DOG BROKER.

PUPS SOLD ON NON-BREEDING CONTRACT
THIS PUP WAS SOLD ON NON-BREEDING CONTRACT YES NO

BUYER AGREES TO SPAY OR NEUTER PUP IF BOUGHT ON NON-BREEDING CONTRACT.

PUP MUST BE ALTERED AT EARLIEST POSSIBLE AGE RECOMMENDED BY BUYER'S VET.

BUYER AGREES NOT TO USE THIS DOG FOR BREEDING PURPOSES.

BUYER AGREES TO NEVER BREED THEIR MASTIFF TO *ANY OTHER BREED , PIT BULL , ROTTWEILER OR CROSS BREED*.

I AGREE AND WILL ABIDE WITH THE TERMS OF THIS CONTRACT
SIGNATURE OF SELLER_____

SIGNATURE OF BUYER _____

DOG SOLD AS OPEN TO BREED.
MALE DOGS,

THE BUYER AGREES THAT THE SELLER SHALL HAVE TWO FREE BREEDINGS TO THE MALE DOG SOLD OPEN IN THIS CONTRACT.

THE BUYER AGREES TO DO A CERTIFICATION ON HIPS AND ELBOWS BEFORE THEY BREED THE DOG TO ANY BITCH EXCEPT SELLER'S. BUYER AGREES NOT TO BREED THE DOG BEFORE THE AGE OF TWO YEARS.

I {name of buyer}_____
AGREE WITH THE CONDITIONS OF THIS OPEN-TO-BREED CONTRACT

SIGNATURE OF BUYER_____

FEMALE SOLD AS OPEN TO BREED
THE BUYER AGREES TO GIVE SELLER ONE FREE PUP FROM THE FIRST LITTER BRED BY THIS FEMALE. PUP SHALL BE THIRD PICK OF LITTER.

IF ONLY TWO OR FEWER PUPS ARE BORN IN THIS FIRST LITTER, BUYER WILL WAIT FOR PUP FROM THE BITCH'S SECOND LITTER.

I {name of buyer_}_____
HEREBY AGREE WITH THIS CONDITION OF THE OPEN-TO-BREED CONTRACT.

SIGNATURE OF BUYER _____

What about rescue groups?

You may decide that, rather than working through a breeder, you want to get a dog from a rescue group. This is probably more of an option for you if you want an adult dog rather than a puppy. There can be several advantages in adopting a mature rescue dog:

- You already know how big the Mastiff will be
- The Mastiff may already be house-trained
- The Mastiff may have already received obedience training
- The Mastiff's basic personality and temperament will already be set
- The Mastiff will already be past the active puppy stage
- The Mastiff will already have been spayed or neutered

Dogs frequently end up as rescue dogs for reasons completely unrelated to their personalities or characteristics as a pet. Reasons include divorce, illness, relocation, or change in economic status. For Mastiffs, owners are often simply unprepared for dealing with such a large dog, and find that it is more than they can handle.

When a dog arrives at a rescue group, it will be evaluated to determine its behavior, temperament, and personality. In addition, applicants who want to adopt a rescue dog are evaluated to ensure that they are suitable dog owners and that the dog they want fits their family, home, and lifestyle.

If you do get a dog from a rescue group, try to get as much information about the dog's past as possible. Why was it given up? Who were its parents? How old is it? Is it healthy? Did it receive any training? Was it around other animals, and if so, did it get along with them? Was it treated well in its former family? All this information will help you integrate the Mastiff into your family more quickly and easily.

What about pet shops?

Can you buy a healthy Mastiff from a pet shop? Possibly, but not likely. It is best to avoid pet shops altogether. Reputable breeders do not sell or consign their animals to pet shops. If you buy an animal from a pet shop, you have no way of knowing your pet's genetic background. In addition, pet shop puppies are probably not well-socialized, are exposed to numerous health risks, and are even harder to housebreak (because they are used to living in a small cage where they have no separate bathroom area).

Chapter 5
PUPPY LOVE: BRINGING HOME YOUR MASTIFF PUPPY

You have chosen your Mastiff puppy and are bringing it home for the first time. How can you help make this transition into the adult world as easy as possible for your new "fur baby?"

Go shopping

Before you bring your puppy home, you need to buy a few things in preparation:

- **A dog crate**. You will eventually need an extra-large one. If you don't want to buy a small one now and a large one later, choose a crate with partitions or one that can be adjusted from puppy-size to adult-size. You can also use cardboard to partition a larger crate.
- **Blankets and bedding**. Even if the puppy sleeps in the crate at night, you may want a pet bed for daytime naps when you are home.
- **Food and water bowls**. Select bowls that won't tip and are easy to clean. You may want to buy smaller bowls at first, and get larger ones as your puppy grows.
- **An adjustable dog collar.** Lightweight nylon or leather collars are best. The collar is the right size when you can comfortably slide two fingers between the collar and your puppy's neck. Remember to attach an identification tag listing your puppy's name and your address and phone number.
- **Leash**. A six-foot leash is the ideal length for training and walking. Most communities have leash laws, so you will need to keep your puppy on a leash whenever it is outside and not in a fenced yard.

Mastiff Secrets

- **Grooming supplies.** You will need a flea comb and a brush with natural bristles, a rubber currycomb, or a hand mitt.
- **Lots of chew toys.** Large rawhide chips, nylon chews, and hard rubber balls are good choices. Anything made of soft rubber, fur, wool, sponge, or plastic can be dangerous, as small pieces can break off and choke the puppy or upset its tummy. Also consider the size of the toy: if it fits comfortably in the puppy's mouth, it is too small.
- **Stain and scent remover.** Potty-training accidents will happen. Buy stain and scent remover in the pet aisle or pet supply store. Look for a product that is formulated to completely remove the urine scent; otherwise, the puppy will keep going in the same spot.
- **Dog food.** For the first couple of weeks, give the puppy the same food it was used to eating at the breeder's.
- **Bottled water.** You will want to give the puppy bottled water for a few days.
- **Drool towels.** Yes, Mastiffs do drool!
- **Doghouse**, if the puppy will be outside during the day.

Puppy-proof your house

Puppies are curious creatures and will explore every nook and cranny of your house. You need to make sure your puppy can explore safely by

- Storing all poisonous household items out of the puppy's range. These include household cleaners, laundry detergents, bleach, disinfectants, insecticides, cleaning fluids, fertilizers, mothballs, antifreeze, insect poisons, and rat poisons. You should also get in the habit of keeping the toilet lid down so the puppy doesn't accidentally get a drink of toilet cleaner.
- Put all poisonous plants out of the puppy's range. Following is a partial list of plants that are potentially dangerous to animals:

  - Aloe Vera
  - Amaryllis
  - Asparagus Fern
  - Autumn Crocus
  - Azalea
  - Caladium
  - Calla Lily
  - Castor Bean
  - Chinese Evergreen
  - Cineraria
  - Clematis
  - Philodendron
  - Cyclamen
  - Daffodil
  - Dieffenbachia
  - Elephant Ears
  - Ivy
  - Eucalyptus
  - Geranium
  - Lily
  - Lily of the Valley
  - Mistletoe
  - Morning Glory
  - Narcissus
  - Nightshade
  - Oleander
  - Onion
  - Plumosa Fern

- Poinsettia
- Primrose
- Rhododendron
- Sago Palm
- Tomato Plant (green fruit, stem and leaves)
- Yew

- Get down on all fours and look at your house from your puppy's point of view. Are there loose nails, plastic bags, or dangling electrical or blind cords that your puppy can get into? Remove or move anything that looks hazardous to your puppy.
- If you have a balcony, high deck, porch, or loft, make sure the puppy can't get to those areas unsupervised or install shielding so the puppy can't slip through the banister openings and fall
- Make sure there are no sharp objects such as pins, needles, or thumbtacks on the floor or anywhere your puppy could get them and swallow them.

Prepare a place for the new puppy

Just like all new babies, your puppy needs a lot of sleep. Have a bed, a blanket, a crate, or another private area already prepared for your new companion. Don't let children or anyone else disturb the puppy while it is sleeping. You don't want a cranky, sleep-deprived puppy!

Teach the house rules

Like adult Mastiffs, Mastiff puppies tend to be calmer than other puppies. But they are still puppies, and they will be active! Teach your puppy the house rules from the beginning — where to sleep, where to eat, what furniture or rooms are off-limits, etc. Be gentle, firm, and consistent. Never yell at or hit your puppy.

Be available

Mastiffs are social creatures and they need a great deal of affection and company. Your puppy will need to learn to trust you before it will feel safe in its new home. Try not to leave your puppy alone for long periods of time when it is still new to the household. However, you can start to teach it about being alone. Give the puppy a favorite toy and then leave the house or the room for a few minutes, returning before the puppy starts crying for you. Each time you leave, stay away a little longer. Your puppy will soon learn that when you leave, you always come back.

Be gentle

Mastiff puppies grow at a tremendous rate, doubling their weight several times over the first few months of their lives. This growth puts a strain on the dog's bones, joints, and muscles. To ensure that your dog grows up healthy and strong, take slow daily walks that are not too long. Don't walk any farther than you can comfortably carry your puppy back, should it get tired or worn out.

Play with your dog gently, and don't let it exert its full strength until it is fully grown, at about three years old. Don't let it play roughly with other dogs or your children. A Mastiff can be permanently damaged by overexertion at a young age.

Schedule an appointment with your vet

Your new puppy should have had its first set of vaccinations and have been wormed by the breeder before you picked it up. However, it will need booster shots two weeks and six months after its first vaccination. Until then, your puppy is not fully protected from diseases such as parvovirus.

To help keep your puppy safe until the full round of vaccinations is complete, follow these tips:

- Keep your puppy away from public places where other dogs may have been. This includes parks, walking trails, and the street.
- Don't let your puppy sniff or play with strange dogs.
- Don't let your puppy eat from a dish that another dog has used.

In addition to the booster shots, your puppy will also need to be wormed again when you go to the vet. Request that your vet use a broad spectrum wormer to protect your puppy against all worms.

Feeding your Mastiff puppy

Moving to a new home away from its mother and littermates is stressful for a puppy and can lead to an upset tummy. To help make the transition easier on your puppy, feed it only the food recommended by the breeder for at least the first two weeks. In addition to helping the puppy feel secure, this will also help if the puppy gets sick: you will know the illness is not from a change in diet.

After a couple of weeks, you can start mixing in your choice of food with the brand the puppy is used to. You can also offer the puppy cow bones, chew toys, and nylon chew bones.

A change in water can also upset your puppy's tummy. To keep it feeling its best, offer only bottled water for the first week. After this, you can begin mixing bottled water with tap water, gradually reducing the amount of bottled water.

The first day and night in a new home

The first night away from its old home and familiar surroundings can be the hardest on a puppy. To help your puppy adjust to its new family, follow these tips:

- Ask the breeder for a blanket or toy that has been in the puppy's bed and smells like its mother and littermates. The scent will help your puppy feel more secure and less lonely.
- Pick up your puppy at the beginning of a weekend. If you can, add a few vacation days as well. The more time you have to spend with your Mastiff puppy in the beginning, the better.
- Pick your puppy up in the morning so you can spend the whole day bonding and getting to know each other before bedtime.
- When you get home, immediately take your puppy outside to the area you want it to use as a bathroom.
- Caution children to be calm and gentle with the puppy, which will be feeling overwhelmed. Teach them the proper way to play with and hold the puppy, and also teach them to leave the puppy alone when it is sleeping.
- At bedtime, put the puppy in his crate. The puppy will probably cry the first few nights. If you can, put the crate near your bed, so the puppy will know you are there and you can pat it through the crate door when it cries. If you find yourself losing patience, however, move the crate to the other end of the house where you can't hear the cries. Never yell at or scold the puppy for crying. Sometimes, putting a cloth over the front of the crate helps the puppy relax and fall asleep.

Chapter 6
DIET AND GROOMING TIPS

Feeding and grooming your Mastiff will help it stay healthy and happy.

Diet

Your Mastiff's dietary needs will change as it grows larger and older.

The puppy years

During their growing years (up to age three or four), Mastiffs need a lot of food. They are growing very quickly and might gain as much as five pounds in one week. This is especially true in their first year of life.

When you get your puppy, the breeder will give you a diet sheet listing everything the puppy has been eating and how many meals it has been getting. To avoid digestive upsets, don't make any sudden changes to your puppy's diet. Stick with a good quality, balanced diet. Feeding your Mastiff foods that are too high in protein, calories, and fat will make it grow too fast, possibly causing joint, ligament, and tendon problems.

Mastiff puppies tend to overeat and get bloated, so don't leave food out for them all the time. Instead, feed your puppy two or three small meals a day rather than one large meal.

Adult dogs

Once fully grown, Mastiffs require less food than you would think. In fact, because they tend to be relatively inactive, they eat about the same as a medium-size active dog such as a German shepherd.

What food to choose

Select a good quality premium food. Yes, this will cost more in the short term than a bag of low-quality food from the grocery store. However, your Mastiff will eat more of the low-quality food because it is less nutritiously dense — and there goes your savings. (In addition, dogs tend to be gassier when they eat low-quality food).

Mastiffs do best on a food that is in the medium range for protein (20-25%), and mid-range for fat (12-18%), is well balanced for calcium and phosphorus, and is high in iodine (3-5%).

Another alternative is to provide your Mastiff a "real food" diet. This means giving your dog foods such as fresh chicken, turkey, beef; oatmeal; yogurt; and eggs. You can find recipes for making your own dog food on the Internet (www.bc-mastiffs.com/bcenglishmastiffsnutritionandhealth.html).

How much food?

The amount of food you give your Mastiff is a judgment call, depending on

- The type of food you are feeding
- Your Mastiff's age
- Your Mastiff's body condition (too fat, too thin or just right)

Follow the recommendations on the food bag and adjust the amount according to your dog's body condition. You should be able to feel your Mastiff's ribs and see at least the last two ribs when it is moving. If you can't feel and see the ribs, your dog is getting fat, and you need to reduce the amount of food.

A grown-up bowl

As your Mastiff grows, you will also want to invest in elevated bowls for both food and water. This will make eating more comfortable for your dog.

Water

Mastiffs drink a lot of water each day and they can become distressed very quickly if water is not available. Make sure your mastiff has fresh water available at all times, and change the water in its bowl at least once a day.

Bones

For a special treat for your Mastiff, get a large, solid bone from the grocery store or butcher. These are often available at low cost, or even free. When the meat is gone, you can boil the bone in bouillon to add some more taste and smell.

Bone like this are not only yummy treats, they are good for your dog's teeth.

Grooming

Because Mastiffs are short-haired, they are relatively easy to groom. Grooming includes activities such as

- Bathing
- Brushing
- Cleaning eyes and ears
- Clipping toenails

You obviously won't do all of these things every day, but you should brush your dog and check its ears every day.

Starting early

Teach your Mastiff to stand still for brushing and other grooming while it is still a puppy. This habit will definitely make grooming easier when your puppy weighs as much as you do!

Your puppy may not like grooming at first, but if you are gentle, calm, and consistent, it will soon begin to enjoy spending this time with you. Don't use force if the puppy seems to find grooming scary. Allow your puppy time to get used to grooming by brushing just a few minutes the first week or two, and then gradually increasing the time.

Bathing

Regular baths will help your Mastiff smell better and will reduce its shedding. This does not mean you should bathe your Mastiff daily or even weekly — too much bathing is bad for its skin. Once every month or so is enough unless it starts to smell too much in the meantime.

When you bathe your dog, it is important to use dog shampoo. People shampoo will ruin your dog's coat and can lead to eczema and rashes.

Where can you bathe such a big dog? The bathtub actually does work, although a Mastiff will probably fill the tub. If the weather is warm enough, you can use a large plastic or metal tub outdoors. Some pet stores even have booths where you can take your dog and wash it yourself. Of course, the store will be glad to wash your pet for you, but it will cost more than just renting the booth.

Brushing

You should brush your Mastiff every day. Dust, dead hair, and dandruff stay in the Mastiff's coat until you brush it out. Regular brushing improves your dog's odor, reduces shedding, and prevents skin infections.

There are several choices for brushing a short-haired dog such as a Mastiff:

- Dog glove
- Firm bristle-brush
- Rubber brush

You can even "brush" your Mastiff without any tools at all. Just get your hands wet and then "brush" forward from tail to head. Rinse your hands and then "brush" again, this time from head to tail.

After you brush your Mastiff, rub it with a chamois or other cloth to make its coat shiny.

Cleaning ears

You should clean your dog's ears regularly to prevent infections and mites. The insides of Mastiffs' ears don't dry very well, which means their ear wax stays moist. This provides an ideal breeding ground for mites, as well as for bacteria that can cause unpleasant, painful, and smelly ear infections.

Wash your Mastiff's ears with a soft dry cloth. Do not use a Q-tip or anything that could push the wax further into the ears. Just wipe the parts of the ear you can see with the cloth, and you are done!

Cleaning eyes

Some Mastiffs tend to get a lot of mess in their eyes, especially if they have a lot of loose skin on their face or around their eyes. This not only looks ugly, it can also lead to eye infections.

You don't need to have a regular time to clean your Mastiff's eyes; just look them over occasionally, especially in the morning or after a long nap, and clean them as necessary. You will soon learn whether your Mastiff seems to need cleaning more often.

To clean your Mastiff's eyes, use a wet, soft cloth to very gently wipe the eye from the inside edge outward. Be gentle and careful; you could irritate the eye even more if you wipe too hard.

Clipping toenails

Nail clipping is probably the most intimidating grooming task because if you do it wrong, it can hurt your Mastiff and make it bleed quite a bit. You can pay to have your Mastiff's toenails clipped, but this can be expensive, especially if you are doing it every week. If you are careful, there is no reason you cannot successfully clip your own Mastiff's nails.

You should clip your Mastiff's toenails once a week. If you let them go too long, walking becomes uncomfortable and the nails become harder to clip.

To clip your Mastiff's nails, you will need clippers made for dogs. These come in different sizes; you will need the largest size. Then, follow these steps to clip those claws:

1. Make the dog stand still.
2. Lift up a front leg and take a close look at the back of one of the toenails. You should be able to see the nerve (also called the quick). This is a black line inside the toenail. It is shorter than the full length of the claw.
3. With the clippers, cut the toenail. Do not cut as far as the quick or you will hurt your dog. It's better to cut off too little than too much.

Other grooming

In addition to these regular grooming needs, your Mastiff also benefits from

- Regular tooth-brushing
- Clipping the hair between the pads of the feet

Chapter 7
KEEPING YOUR MASTIFF HEALTHY

As with most giant breeds, Mastiffs have a relatively short life expectancy, living about 6-10 years. What can you do to make those years healthy and happy? This chapter will tell you how.

Exercise

Mastiffs are inclined to be lazy, but they will be healthier and happier if they receive regular exercise. So take walks together, play fetch and other games, and keep your Mastiff trim and healthy.

Remember that you should NOT overexercise a Mastiff puppy. Until a Mastiff is around three years old, its skeleton is still developing. Too much exercise can lead to permanent damage.

When you do begin to exercise your Mastiff, begin gradually and build up slowly. Keep an eye out for signs that your dog is getting tired or overheated. If you are on a walk or away from home, always carry water with you, as Mastiffs get very thirsty.

Playtime

A great way to keep your Mastiff active is to have a regular playtime. Playing with your Mastiff will keep it healthy and make it happy, because it loves nothing better than spending time with you.

When playing with your Mastiff, try to do things it enjoys. If your Mastiff enjoys running, play fetch and let it run after a ball or Frisbee. If it likes water, squirt it gently with a hose or fill a small pool with water and romp together.

When you play, be sure to set some ground rules for your Mastiff so YOU can stay healthy too. Remember, your playmate just may outweigh you! Let your Mastiff know what activities are okay and what activities are not okay. For example, maybe it is okay if the Mastiff gently grabs your arm, but not okay if it bites or nips. In addition, if children are also playing, it is not even okay for the Mastiff to grab a child's arm. Your Mastiff should be able to understand the meaning of "Careful," "Gentle," "No," or whatever words you use to direct the playtime, and it should understand that children receive gentler treatment than adults do.

If you are going to get toys for your Mastiff, good choices include large chew bones and balls. Of course, plain old sticks from the backyard are always popular toys, too, and they have the advantage of being free.

Common health problems

Although Mastiffs are prone to a variety of genetic disorders, the most common reasons for poor health in a Mastiff are accidents, injuries, and poor nutrition. Feed your Mastiff well and keep it safe, and you greatly improve its chances for a long healthy life.

Most breeders test for genetic faults in their breeding programs, which in return ensure you a healthy new family member with their health guarantee built into your purchase contract.

Progressive Retinal Atrophy

Progressive Retinal Atrophy (PRA) is an inherited eye disease affecting the retina that ultimately results in blindness. Typically, the first symptom of PRA is night blindness, followed by a "green sheen" to the eyes when viewed in dim light.

Mastiffs now have a DNA gene test. Before the dog is old enough to develop symptoms, breeders send in a blood sample, which is used to determine whether a dog has PRA, is a carrier of PRA, or is clear (has none of the genes for PRA). Once breeders have this information, they can plan breedings that will not produce any pups with PRA.

Hip Dysplasia

Hip dysplasia is a crippling joint disease and is one of the most common health problems in Mastiffs. Although it is primarily an inherited defect, the severity of the disease is affected by your Mastiff's growth rate, diet, and exercise.

There is not yet a DNA test to identify dogs likely to get hip dysplasia, but there are several screening techniques that breeders can use.

To help prevent hip dysplasia in your Mastiff, follow these tips:

- Maintain a slow growth rate for your puppy as it grows up.
- Keep your Mastiff active so it maintains good muscle tone.
- Do not allow your Mastiff to become overweight.

Many surgical and non-surgical treatments are available for hip dysplasia. Talk to your veterinarian about the best options for you and your Mastiff.

A form of dysplasia can also affect your Mastiff's elbow.

Hypothyroidism

Hypothyroidism occurs when the thyroid gland does not produce enough thyroid hormone. Symptoms include mental dullness, lethargy, change in hair color or luster, infertility, slow heart rate, and abnormal heartbeat.

The only way to know whether your Mastiff has hypothyroidism is to have it tested. If the tests are positive, thyroid replacement therapy is available to get your Mastiff's hormone levels back to normal.

Osteochrondritis Dissecans (OCD)

In Osteochrondritis Dissecans, a lesion occurs in a Mastiff's joint. This causes a flap of cartilage to become loose, exposing the nerves in the underlying bone and causing great pain. Surgery is usually required.

OCD probably has a basis in heredity, but stress and nutrition also play a role. Wight control and good nutrition can help to prevent this disease, as can avoiding rough play during the first year of life.

Arthritis

Arthritis is a common disorder in Mastiffs, as it is in all large dogs. Symptoms range from mild lameness to total non-weight bearing of the affected limb. Anti-inflammatory medicine can be used to treat the arthritis, or surgery can be performed to replace the degenerated joint.

Arthritis may be genetically related and can be triggered by poor nutrition, trauma, aging, and obesity. To prevent or slow the progress of arthritis, make sure to provide nutritious food and don't let your Mastiff become overweight.

Bloat

Bloat is a common disorder to Mastiffs. It occurs when gas builds up in a dog's digestive system and the dog cannot dispel it. Bloat is a life-threatening illness — see the next chapter for how to treat bloat.

To prevent bloat, try the following tips:

- Feed your Mastiff two or three small meals a day instead of one large meal.
- Do not allow your Mastiff to drink large quantities of water at one time. Instead, have water available all the time so your Mastiff never gets too thirsty.
- Do not exercise your Mastiff for at least two hours after a full meal. Conversely, don't feed your Mastiff immediately after exercising.
- Feed a diet composed of more meats and less grain.
- Keep your dog at a normal weight.
- If your Mastiff is nervous and shy, feed it in a quiet, relaxed atmosphere.
- Change your dog's diet slowly.

Elbow and knee bursas

A bursa is a protective swelling around the elbow and knee joints. It begins as a fluid-filled pocket and eventually develops into a rough pad.

Mastiffs develop bursas because they use their elbows and knees to lever their large bodies off the ground. Bursas can be surgically removed, but if they are not causing your Mastiff any pain, you may choose to leave them.

Cruciate Knee Rupture

Cruciate knee injuries are common to Mastiffs. When Mastiffs play hard, they can rupture the ligament of their knees, becoming lame in the affected limb. If the ligament is only strained, confinement can allow it to heal. However, if the ligament is torn, surgery will be required or the joint will develop arthritis.

Chapter 8
FIRST AID FOR YOUR MASTIFF

In an emergency, you need to get your Mastiff to a veterinarian as quickly as possible. However, knowing how to provide basic first aid can help your Mastiff survive until you get to the vet. This chapter tells you how to be prepared for emergencies and lists some common emergencies, how to recognize them, and what you can do.

Choose a vet

You should already have a veterinarian with whom you feel comfortable. The veterinarian should provide you with advice and care about your animal, be willing to answer your questions, help you understand your pet, and be willing to see you in emergencies or refer you to an emergency clinic or hospital.

Keep good records

You should always have updated shot records and medical histories for your pets. This information will be especially important if you are referred to an emergency clinic where the veterinarian has never seen your pet.

Evaluating your Mastiff's condition

If you call your veterinarian or emergency hospital, the staff will ask you about your dog's condition. Here are some basic tests you can do to evaluate how your Mastiff is doing:

Capillary refill time

Capillary refill time measures blood flow through the body. To test your Mastiff's capillary refill time, roll its lip back and press on a non-pigmented area of the gums with one finger. The area should turn from pink to almost white. Once you remove your finger, the pink color should return in one to two seconds.

Respiration

Watch or feel the Mastiff's chest rise and fall. Count the number of breaths for 15 seconds, and then multiply by four to figure out the respirations per minute. Normal respiratory rate should be 10 to 30 respirations per minute.

Pulse

To feel your Mastiff's heartbeat, place a hand over its chest or place your first two fingers on the inside part of its thigh. Note whether the heartbeats feel strong or weak.

Now count the heartbeats for 15 seconds, and then multiply by four to figure out the heartbeats per minute. Normal pulse should be 60 to 120 beats per minute.

Temperature

To take your Mastiff's temperature, insert a rectal thermometer (one with a rounded end bulb) into its rectum for 1 minute. Normal temperature should be 101-102 degrees F.

Hydration

To determine whether your Mastiff is dehydrated, pick up the skin on the scruff of the neck and let it go. If it immediately returns back into place, the dog is not dehydrated. If it is slow to return into place, the animal is dehydrated.

For puppies, you can assess their dehydration by looking at their urine. The urine should be as clear as water or light yellow. Dark yellow urine is a sign of dehydration.

Mastiff Secrets

Dealing with emergencies

Shock

Often when your Mastiff is ill or injured, it will go into shock. You then need to treat the dog for both the initial injury/illness and for shock.

Shock occurs when an animal's cardiovascular system doesn't provide body tissues with enough oxygen. If your dog is in shock, you will see the following symptoms:

- Gums/lips are pale and dry
- Pulse is weak and rapid
- Breathing is irregular, shallow, and rapid
- Pupils are dilated
- Skin and legs feel cool

The dog may also collapse or go unconscious.

If your Mastiff goes into shock, you need to keep it quiet and warm. Wrap it in blankets and put it in a heated car to go to the veterinarian.

Bloat

Bloat occurs when gas builds up in a dog's digestive system and the dog is unable to dispel it. Bloat is very dangerous. It can occur quickly and needs to be treated immediately.

Common symptoms of bloat include:

- Major anxiety
- Abdominal swelling after meals
- Gagging
- Whining
- Heavy salivating
- Pacing
- Dry vomiting
- Heavy panting
- Shallow breathing
- Restlessness
- Rapid heartbeat
- Weak pulse
- Blue, dark red, or white gums

When bloat begins, your Mastiff will not be interested in food or water. Then, after 30-60 minutes, its midsection will begin to swell as gas accumulates in the stomach. The Mastiff will then begin to pant heavily and breathe rapidly.

If you suspect your dog has bloat, get it to the vet or an emergency hospital IMMEDIATELY.

Overeating

Mastiffs of all ages will overeat if food is available to them all the time. However, this illness is more common in puppies or in dogs that do not eat regular meals. Also note that although you may limit your dog's food intake, it may find something else to snack on, such as garbage.

Too much water can also lead to an overly full stomach, especially if your Mastiff drinks a lot of water after eating dry food or exercising.

Symptoms of overeating include a swollen abdomen, retching, and vomiting. If your Mastiff is also having any problems breathing, get it to a veterinarian immediately.

To treat a case of overeating, don't let your Mastiff have any more food or water for a while. Keep it quiet and make sure it gets lots of fresh air.

Gastric Dilation/Volvulus

As with bloat, volvulus occurs when gas accumulates in the stomach. However, with volvulus, the stomach twists. Shock, coma, and death can occur in two to three hours.

Symptoms of volvulus include:

- Enlarged abdomen
- Painful abdomen, especially when touched
- Excess salivation
- Unsuccessful attempts to vomit
- Difficulty breathing
- Either refusal to lie down, or lying down and refusal to move

If your Mastiff shows these symptoms, get it to a vet or emergency hospital IMMEDIATELY.

External bleeding

If your Mastiff is injured and bleeding, you should first try to control the bleeding by applying a pressure bandage. Put a clean piece of gauze or cloth directly over the wound and secure it with torn strips of cloth, masking tape, or whatever else you have available. If nothing else is available, use your hands to hold the cloth in place. Bleeding from minor cuts and wounds should stop within a few minutes

If the bleeding will not stop, you can apply a tourniquet. This should be a last resort for severe injuries. To make a tourniquet, use a two-inch wide gauze bandage or cloth and tie it directly above the wound. Don't tie the tourniquet too tightly: you should still be able to place a finger under it. Also, untie the tourniquet every 10 minutes.

Bleeding from specific parts of the body requires special treatment:

Ear

An ear injury often does not clot because the ear moves when the Mastiff shakes its head. To keep the ear still, bind it to the head with gauze or tape or use a nylon or knee sock with the bottom cut out.

Footpad

Apply a pressure bandage to a bleeding footpad.

Penis

A female in heat will excite the male and can cause uncontrollable hemorrhaging from the penis. Remove the male from the area and apply cold compresses to the penis.

Toenail

If you clip a toenail too short, it can bleed quite a bit. If this occurs, have the dog lie down to relieve pressure on the foot. Then put the bleeding nail into a wet bar of soap. Alternatively, you can make a mush by mixing flour or baking soda with water and putting it on the nail. If the bleeding still won't stop, apply a loose bandage.

Internal bleeding

If your Mastiff has been hit by a car or suffered a blow to the chest, internal bleeding is a definite possibility. Get your Mastiff to a veterinarian as soon as possible. DO not give it anything to eat or drink.

Signs of internal bleeding include the following:

- Coughing up bright red, foamy blood
- Vomit with bright red or dark reddish-brown blood
- Pale gums
- Panting

Choking

Choking can occur when objects such as rubber balls or pieces of meat lodge in the back of the throat, blocking breathing. Choking can also be caused by throat swelling due to allergic reactions or infections.

If your dog is choking, it will not be able to breathe, its tongue will turn blue, and it will collapse.

To help a choking dog,

1. Have it lie on its side.
2. Pull the dog's tongue forward and look at the throat. Be careful: the dog will be scared and panicky, and may try to bite you.
3. If you can see and reach anything, carefully remove it.
4. If you can't reach the object, you can try to dislodge it. While the dog is lying down, strike the side of the rib cage with the palm of your hand three to four times. Alternatively, you can stand behind the dog and lift its forelegs while giving three to four forceful compressions on both sides of the chest.

If the choking is caused by an allergic reaction or infection, get your Mastiff to a veterinarian IMMEDIATELY.

Foreign body in the mouth or esophagus

Objects can get stuck in your Mastiff's mouth, and although it can still breathe, it will be uncomfortable and possibly even in pain.

If your Mastiff has something stuck in its throat, it will be gagging, spitting up white or blood-tinged phlegm, pawing at the mouth, and rubbing the side of its head on the ground. To get the object out, press your thumb and forefinger into your Mastiff's upper cheeks, forcing its mouth to open wide. Use your fingers or long-nosed pliers to gently remove the object. Be careful not to push it further down, or you could cause your dog to choke.

If you cannot get the object out, take your Mastiff to a veterinarian.

Convulsions

Convulsions are involuntary muscle contractions. During a convulsion, your Mastiff will look frightened or dazed. It will salivate, shake its head, lick its lips, and snap its jaw. Its pupils will dilate and it will have violent muscle contractions and rapid leg movements. It will also breathe rapidly. Your Mastiff may or may not lose consciousness. When the convulsion ends, the animal will feel disoriented and confused.

During a convulsion, you need to remain calm. All you can do is try to prevent your Mastiff from injuring you or ifself. Try to lay the Mastiff on a blanket on the floor in a quiet area.

If your Mastiff has frequent convulsions, you need to take it to the vet. Also note that poisons are a common cause of convulsions, so consider whether your Mastiff may have gotten into something poisonous. If you think this is a possibility, get it to the veterinarian.

Ear injuries

Ear injuries can be caused by insect bites, infections, and foreign bodies inside the ear canal. If your Mastiff has an ear injury, it will display the following symptoms:

- Violent head shaking
- Scratching at the ears and neck
- Dragging the ear along on the floor
- Tilting the head to one side
- Tenderness when the ear is handled
- Unusual odor
- Discharge from the ear
- Swelling of the ear

If your Mastiff has an infection, you can clip the wound area and apply an antiseptic cream. If you can see a foreign body in the ear canal, you can gently try to remove it.

If the Mastiff seems to be in pain, pour mineral, baby, or olive oil into the ear canal.

Eye injuries

If your Mastiff gets something in its eye or seems to have a scratch or wound on its eye, it needs to be seen by a veterinarian. Eyes are very delicate, and emergency care may be needed to prevent permanent loss of vision.

The one exception to this rule is if there is a foreign object you can easily get out without touching or wiping the eyeball. You can try pouring water or eyewash in the eye to flush out the object.

A Mastiff with an eye injury will display the following symptoms:

- Rubbing and pawing at the face/eyes
- Eye tightly shut
- Eyelids swollen
- Eyes watering
- Eyes sensitive to light

Electrical shock

Curious puppies may be enchanted by electrical cords and bite through them. If this happens, you need to separate the puppy from the electrical source without touching it or using anything that is wet or that conducts electricity. If you can, shut off the current at a circuit breaker or fuse box and unplug the electrical cord. Then use a pole or board to push the puppy away from the cord and take it to a veterinarian.

Allergic reactions

If your dog has a severe allergic reaction to a food, medicine, insect bite, or something else, it can go into shock within one to 15 minutes. It will become restless, and begin to vomit or have diarrhea. In the case of an insect bite, the animal will swell at the bite location.

You must get your Mastiff to a veterinarian immediately for a shot of epinephrine. If necessary, the vet will also establish an airway to ease your dog's breathing and will treat it for shock.

Less severe allergic reactions can lead to hives and swelling. In this milder reaction, your dog will begin swelling anywhere from 10 minutes to several hours after exposure to the allergen. Its face, face, head, lips, ears, and eyelids will swell and the dog may rub its mouth and eyes along the ground.

If you think a chemical caused the reaction, wash the animal free of any residues. You should also place cold packs on insect bites. If your dog seems very uncomfortable, you can give it an antihistamine. Call your vet to find out how much and what brand to give your Mastiff.

Frostbite

If your Mastiff is out in the cold too long, it can become frostbitten. The most common sites for frostbite on a dog are the scrotum, ears, feet, teats, and tail. Signs of frostbite include

- White or grayish tissues
- Shock
- Scaliness of the skin
- Possible sloughing of the surface tissue

Old wives' tales to the contrary, you should never rub or massage frozen tissues, nor should you put snow or ice on them. Instead, put the affected area in warm water or wrap it in warm, moist towels. This will warm it quickly. Once the tissues begin to look flushed, dry them off, wrap them in a clean, dry bandage, and take your Mastiff to the veterinarian.

Hit by a car

Car accidents are probably the most common cause of injury for dogs. If your Mastiff is hit by a car, take these steps:

1. Calm the animal down as much as possible. Be careful, because it will be scared and panicky and may bite.
2. If the dog is walking, note whether it is limping and then try to get it to lie down.
3. Evaluate the dog's condition and treat it as necessary for shock and bleeding.
4. Get the dog to a veterinarian.

The size of a Mastiff makes it hard to transport when it is injured. If your Mastiff can't walk, try putting it on a board or in a blanket to carry.

Chapter 9
SOCIALIZING AND TRAINING THE MASTIFF

Because they grow up to be such large dogs and are sensitive and shy, socializing and training your Mastiff is crucial. It may be cute to see a puppy dragging its owner for a walk, but it won't be so cute when the puppy is a 150-pound adult dog.

To find obedience and socialization classes, ask your local Kennel Clubs and veterinarians. Many large pet supply stores also offer obedience and socialization classes.

Socialization

Socialization is an extremely important part of a puppy's training. An unsocialized Mastiff can become both fearful and aggressive, while a well-socialized Mastiff will be stable and confident. Because of their great sensitivity, Mastiffs that are not well socialized when young can become shy of strange people, places, and animals.

A puppy acquires almost all of its sensory, motor, and learning abilities by the time it is 12 weeks old. What your Mastiff puppy learns about people and its environment during these early weeks of life will stay with it for the rest of its life. The more time you spend together playing and cuddling, the stronger the bond you and your Mastiff will develop.

Grooming can also be a special time to strengthen your bond. Brush your pup and wipe its ears every day. If it fusses, say "no" firmly, and when it stands quietly, talk to it in a soft, pleasant voice.

Part of socialization involves just taking your puppy out often to places where it can meet people and other dogs in a friendly atmosphere. As soon as your puppy has had all its shots and your veterinarian says it is safe, you should begin exposing your puppy to as much of the outside world as possible. Try to visit at least three new places a week and introduce your puppy to five new people at each place. People tend to be fascinated by Mastiffs, so it should not be hard to meet this many people! Also take your puppy on regular car rides.

Around 8-11 weeks old, your Mastiff may go through a "scared" stage, during which time it can easily develop phobias. Stay away from crowds and noisy places during these weeks. If something does frighten your puppy, reassure it in a calm and cheerful voice. Your puppy will sense feelings from you, so downplay the whole experience. Too much attention to a frightening experience may actually encourage a phobia.

Obedience training

Basic obedience training should be a part of every Mastiff's upbringing. It is best to begin training your Mastiff when it is a puppy. A puppy's brain develops very rapidly and the animal absorbs new information quickly and easily. An older dog will also be more lethargic and resistant to the necessary repetitiveness of training. To keep your Mastiff interested in training, work with it several times each day, but no more than 10-15 minutes each time.

Mastiffs are also very sensitive and will not respond to training if they are frightened, hurt, or confused. Be consistent and firm but do not raise your voice or use any kind of physical punishment with your Mastiff. To show your dog that you are dissatisfied with its behavior, tell it "No!" in a firm voice and lead it back to its position. The mastiff wants positive attention from you. If it doesn't get that, it realizes that it didn't do what you wanted it to and it will try harder next time. When it does do the exercise right and receives lots of praise, it will try to make you happy again as soon as it gets the chance.

Most Mastiffs are easy to train because they are so eager to please. Of course, some individual Mastiffs will be stubborn or dominant and will resist training. Make training like a game and use a happy, excited voice. In addition, lots of hugs and plenty of praise should motivate even the most stubborn Mastiff. Make the animal feel appreciated and successful.

In addition to praise, you can give food rewards. Don't give a food reward every time, though. Your dog should learn to obey your commands regardless of whether you have a treat in your pocket.

Basic commands

Unless you plan to compete in conformation or obedience, a basic obedience class is all your puppy needs. In this class, it will learn basic commands:

- Sit
- Down
- Stay
- Come

It will also learn to walk on a leash and will receive some helpful socialization.

Mastiffs do not need protection training. They are naturally protective of their family. Even the gentlest Mastiff will protect its family if it is well socialized and bonded to them.

Although you will certainly want to enroll your puppy in an obedience course, you can also work on training at home.

If you're having trouble getting your Mastiff puppy to obey your commands, examine your technique:

- Are you using its name to get its attention before giving a command?
- Are you squatting to its level?
- Are you using an enthusiastic voice?
- Are giving immediate praise?
- Are you practicing?

Sit

By eight weeks of age, your Mastiff puppy is ready to learn to sit. "Sit" is an excellent command to teach a puppy. Once your puppy realizes that sitting is a sure way to receive praise, you will never have to worry about your puppy jumping on you or other people.

To teach your puppy to sit,

1. Get your puppy's attention.
2. Say your puppy's name and then say "Sit" while you gently fold its back legs under its rump to help it into a sitting position.
3. Praise it profusely and offer a treat.

Repeat these steps often and soon your Mastiff will be sitting at your command.

Down

Use the same basic procedure to teach your Mastiff "Down" as you did for teaching "Sit," except that you pull its forelegs forward and down (it may be easier to do this if your Mastiff is already sitting). Say "Down" as you do this, and of course praise your pet profusely once it is down. It can also be helpful to make a downward motion with your hand as you say "Down."

Stay

Once your dog knows and obeys the commands "Sit" and "Down," you can teach "Stay." "Stay" is a very important command to know in everyday life. You must be able to stop your Mastiff from running into the road and getting into other dangerous situations.

To teach your Mastiff to stay,

1. Start by telling your dog to sit.
2. When it sits, say "Stay."
3. While holding an open hand towards your Mastiff, take a couple of steps away from him.
4. If it gets up, say "No!" and lead it back into position.
5. Repeat "Stay" and move away again.
6. Stand still a few seconds and then go back to the dog.
7. Praise and reward your Mastiff for a job well done.

Your Mastiff should stand still and wait until you release it from the command. Gradually increase how far you move away and how long it takes you to walk back to the animal.

Come

You should start teaching your Mastiff the "Come" command the first day you bring it home. Say its name first and then say "Come" in an enthusiastic voice. Praise your pet generously when it comes to you. If it doesn't come immediately, give a tug on its leash to guide it to you.

Leash training

If your Mastiff pulls on the leash during a walk, you probably won't have a very relaxing walk. Your Mastiff is so strong that it could literally pull you off your feet. Therefore, you need to teach it to walk on your left side with its head even with your knee. Start teaching this while the Mastiff still is a puppy.

To get your puppy used to the leash, begin by having it wear a collar. It may resist at first, but do not give in; your puppy must wear a collar for its own safety.

Once the puppy is used to the collar, begin putting it on a leash to take it outside to go potty. Your Mastiff will soon love the leash because it associates it with going outside.

Once your Mastiff puppy is used to the leash, you can introduce the "Heel" command. Get your puppy used to walking on your left side by placing it there every time you put it on the leash. As you walk, talk to your puppy and try to keep it focused on you. When it becomes distracted and runs ahead, call its name, say "Heel," and turn around. The puppy will end up behind you and will hurry to catch up. Praise your pet when it ends up back in position and continue your walk.

Housetraining

Another aspect of training is housetraining. To housetrain your Mastiff quickly, follow these tips:

1. Start by establishing a "bathroom area" in the yard. Always take your puppy to this same area.
2. Each morning, put your Mastiff on the leash and take it to the bathroom area.
3. Use the "potty" command you have selected (potty, hurry up, go now, etc.)
4. After the dog goes potty, bring it inside for food and water.
5. About 15 to 20 minutes after the meal, take the dog outside again for another visit to the bathroom.
6. Take your Mastiff outside regularly throughout the day. You may want to keep it in its crate or on a leash with you at all times. This will help you be sensitive to when the puppy needs to go outside, and also allow you to immediately catch any accidents and get it outside.

It will also help if you maintain a regular schedule for feeding, drinking, and bathroom breaks.

If your Mastiff does have an accident inside, do not yell at or scold it. Hopefully, you have caught it "in the act" and can immediately get it outside to the bathroom area. Be sure you clean the accident area with a pet odor neutralizer so your dog won't think this is a new and convenient inside bathroom area.

Chapter 10
BREEDING YOUR MASTIFF

Choosing to breed your Mastiff is a major decision. You need to consider the health of your Mastiff, test for any genetic conditions that shouldn't be passed on, and choose a mate. If the female is your dog, you must also be prepared to care for a pregnant Mastiff and, eventually, her pups.

Are you ready for breeding?
Before you decide to breed your Mastiff, make sure you have thought about these questions:

- Is your dog a good example of the breed? If you aren't sure, see whether you can have a judge look your Mastiff over. You should not breed your Mastiff just for "fun" or as a money-making venture, but because you want to contribute to the improvement of the Mastiff line.
- If an emergency occurs and your Mastiff needs a Caesarean section, do you have the funds to pay for it?
- Do you have the energy to take care of puppies? If the female Mastiff develops any complications, the puppies will need to be raised by hand. This means bottle-feeding every two to four hours around the clock for about three weeks, until the puppies are weaned.
- Do you have the facilities to accommodate a litter of active puppies? You could have six to 10 puppies in your home — they do not take up much room at birth, but by three weeks old, they already need a large area to live in.
- Will you be able to find suitable homes for the puppies?

Is your female ready for breeding?

A female who is going to be bred needs to be

- Healthy
- The right age — between 22 months and seven years old
- The right weight — if she is overweight, she will have trouble both conceiving and delivering
- Up-to-date on her shots
- Wormed
- Tested for brucellosis and Canine Herpes Virus
- Tested for genetic disorders such as Progressive Retinal Atrophy, hip dysplasia, and elbow dysplasia

In addition, she should not have already been bred within the past year.

Choosing a breeding partner

If you do decide to breed your Mastiff, you need to choose a breeding partner. Do not just plan to use a friend's or neighbor's dog: you need to carefully choose a mate that will complement your Mastiff's characteristics.

A good plan is to first talk with a breeder. Hopefully you have a good relationship with the breeder from whom you bought your Mastiff, and you can start there. Otherwise, try asking the local Kennel Club for names of breeders. A breeder can help you study the temperament, pedigrees, and offspring of potential mates. Look objectively at your Mastiff's faults and make sure you choose a mate who does not share those faults. Two related dogs can be bred.

The owner of the stud should always meet the female dog before the breeding occurs — in fact, before the female is in season. You should also have the breeding contract worked out in advance. This should include any fee arrangements. The contract specifies who pays for what, what the stud fee is, and when it must be paid.

It is also a good idea for female dog owners to have a backup stud, in case their first choice is unavailable when the female actually comes into season.

The breeding environment

Most female dogs come into season around every six months and are ready to breed between the 12th and 15th days. It is a good practice to breed the animals twice, with a day of rest in between.

Breeding can be very stressful for dogs. Some male dogs have even been known to develop bloat when around a female in heat. To reduce the stress, follow these tips:

- Make sure the breeding area is quiet, private, and out of direct sunlight.
- Do not feed the dogs for a few hours before or after the breeding.
- In summer, schedule the breeding for early morning or late evening, when it is cooler outside.
- After the breeding is over, offer the animals a little water or crushed ice and then let them rest in a cool, quiet place.

Caring for the pregnant female

It can be difficult to tell whether a Mastiff is pregnant. At about five weeks, her nipples may swell and her rib cage expand, but this will also occur during false pregnancies. After about seven to eight weeks, you should be able to see the fetuses moving. If you are in any doubt, the veterinarian can perform an ultrasound to verify pregnancy.

During pregnancy, life for a Mastiff continues much the same as usual. You may need to take shorter but more frequent walks so as not to tire her out, and you will also want to start giving her puppy food in order to increase her protein levels.

Time for puppies

The normal length of pregnancy for a Mastiff is 58-67 days after the mating. Indicators that a Mastiff is nearing delivery include

- Drop in body temperature (down to around 98 degrees)
- Enlarged abdomen
- Mammary development
- Loss of appetite
- Behavioral changes
- Drop in progesterone levels

Mastiff Secrets

- Nesting behavior
- Panting
- Vomiting bile

You will want to have a whelping area prepared well in advance. This can be any quiet, warm, draft-free area. Fill the whelping area with easy-to-clean or disposable bedding such as towels and/or newspaper. Encourage her to begin sleeping in the whelping area about a week in advance.

Your Mastiff should be able to deliver the puppies on her own, but you need to stand by to help if necessary. Call your veterinarian when whelping begins in case any complications develop.

Once the puppies are born, make sure the mother removes the bags from their faces so they can breathe. However, do not let the mother eat all the afterbirth or she could get an upset stomach. Use a clean towel to dry the pups and then let them begin to suckle.

Once the whelping is over, put down clean bedding and make sure each puppy has suckled. Then let the mother and puppies rest. Keep the temperature about 95 degrees for the first 36 hours. As soon as the mother will let you, check the puppies for any deformities.

The next day, the new mother will be ready for a light meal such as scrambled eggs. Feed her lightly for the first week; after that, she will need to eat more in order to keep up with the nutritional demands of the puppies. She will especially need high-protein foods, so you can continue to give her puppy food. If she doesn't want to leave her puppies, you can feed her in the whelping box. Don't leave her water in the whelping box, however. You can leave it just outside

If your Mastiff doesn't have enough milk for the puppies, you can bottle-feed them canned goat's milk.

Your veterinarian will want to see the mother shortly after the whelping to make sure everything is okay. She may need a shot of oxycontin or calcium supplements.

Everyone will be excited about the new puppies, but it is best to limit visitors for the first couple of weeks, especially children. Visitors who do come need to be quiet and admire both mother and puppies from afar. Make sure visitors have not been in contact with other dogs, as they could introduce infection to your puppies.

When to call the vet

Your Mastiff should be able to deliver and care for the puppies on her own. However, you need to call your veterinarian right away if —

- She has been straining hard for more than an hour without delivering a puppy. The puppy may be too large or in the wrong position
- After the whelping, she seems weak or restless. She may have retained a puppy.
- Her temperature starts to rise or she gets overly lethargic. She could have a uterine infection.
- She starts to vomit and is shaking or cannot stand up. She could have a calcium deficiency.
- Her discharge is smelly, changes color, or lasts longer than 12 weeks. She could have metritis, a bacterial infection of the uterus.
- A breast becomes swollen, hardened, and painful to the touch. She could have mastitis, a bacterial infection common to Mastiffs.

Mastiff Secrets

Chapter 11
CARING FOR YOUR MASTIFF AS IT AGES

Mastiffs generally live from 8-10 years. You could help your Mastiff's later years be happy and healthy by providing proper nutrition and supplements and scheduling regular visits with your veterinarian.

Nutrition

Healthy mastiffs usually continue to be able to digest and absorb nutrients from their foods, so you don't need to change what they are used to eating. However, an aging Mastiff will become less active and will need fewer calories. If you see your Mastiff starting to gain weight, reduce the amount of food you are giving. If necessary, you can switch to a diet dog food that provides normal levels of protein and other nutrients while decreasing fat and calories.

Obesity is a common problem in aging Mastiffs and can lead to

- Musculoskeletal problems
- Weaker immune system
- Diabetes
- Anesthetic and surgical complications
- Heat and exercise intolerance
- Complications from cardiovascular disease and other diseases

Supplements

Aging mastiffs can benefit from the following nutritional supplements:

- Vitamin C, CoEnzyme Q, and L-carnitine to enhance the immune system, improve overall physical performance, and reduce the incidence and severity of age-related illness
- Unsaturated fatty acids and zinc to maintain healthy coats and skin and help ease arthritis and joint problems

What your veterinarian should check

Mastiffs should have an annual visit with the veterinarian until they are five years old, and biannual visits after that. These visits will help you detect, prevent, and treat some of the common physical problems aging Mastiffs experience.

As your Mastiff ages, your veterinarian should complete the following tests each year:

- Full blood chemistry
- Complete blood count
- Thyroid profile
- Urinalysis
- X-rays of the chest and abdomen
- Ultrasound of the heart and abdomen

These tests will help your veterinarian detect early changes in the heart, kidneys, liver, and other organs as quickly as possible. Although all dog breeds are affected by age, the Mastiff has some special difficulties because of its size.

Cardiac disease

Mastiffs are prone to develop dilative cardiomyopathy (DCM), a heart muscle disease, between four and 10 years old. DCM will eventually lead to congestive heart failure.

Early signs of DCM include

- Loss of appetite
- Weakness
- Coughing
- Loss of interest in exercise

- High blood pressure
- Fluid in the chest or abdomen
- Heart murmur
- Enlarged liver

If DCM is not caught early, your Mastiff can also develop kidney and liver diseases due to lack of sufficient blood in these organs. Treatment may include

- Digoxin, Enalapril, and L-carnitine to help the heart work more efficiently
- Lasix to get rid of the fluid around the lungs and in the abdomen
- CoEnzyme Q to help the cells work better and reduce the impact of low oxygen levels on the heart

Renal disease

Chronic renal failure (CRF) is the most common form of renal disease in Mastiffs. Good nutrition is key to preventing renal failure.

Symptoms of renal failure are typically vague, but may include

- Depression
- Fatigue
- Loss of appetite
- Weight loss
- Frequent urination that is clear like water
- Unusual thirst
- Dehydration
- Poor hair coat

As the kidney disease progresses, your Mastiff will also begin vomiting.

Kidney disease often goes undiagnosed, but if your Mastiff is having annual blood work, your veterinarian should detect it. Many things can cause kidney disease. A veterinarian who suspects kidney disease should do a urinalysis, an ultrasound of the kidneys, and possibly even kidney biopsies.

Long-term treatment for kidney disease will depend on the underlying cause. Initial treatment to save an ill dog may include

- Intensive intravenous fluids to flush the toxins out of the body and stimulate the kidneys to start working again
- Pepcid or tagamet to reduce the stomach upset
- Antibiotics, because the Mastiff's immune system is not working well at this time

- Sodium, potassium, and chloride to hydrate the Mastiff and balance the electrolytes

Gum inflammation and dental disease

Some aging Mastiffs may develop inflamed gums or dental disease. Symptoms include

- Bad breath
- Excessive drooling
- Loss of appetite
- Weight loss
- Pain when trying to eat

It is important to treat dental disorders because bleeding gums allow bacteria around the teeth to gain access to the bloodstream. These bacteria can cause heart disease later.

Try to examine your Mastiff's teeth and gums for unusual redness or swelling. If the Mastiff is in a great deal of pain when you touch its mouth, your veterinarian may need to sedate or anesthetize it. The animal hopefully just needs its teeth cleaned and polished and some antibiotics. Your veterinarian should be able to do this. However, if the disease appears more progressed, your veterinarian may refer you to a veterinarian dentistry specialist.

Adult-onset megaesophagus

In a Mastiff with adult-onset megaesophagus, the esophagus loses its ability to propel food down to the stomach. The food sits in the esophagus despite repeated swallowing attempts. Your Mastiff will eventually start to lose weight because of the lack of food and can develop pneumonia from aspirating food into the lungs.

Adult-onset megaesophagus is often related to other disorders, such as myasthenia gravis, lupus, hypothyroidism, and post-GDV (gastric dilatation-volvulus) syndrome. Therefore, long-term treatment usually includes treating these related disorders. In addition, your veterinarian will likely prescribe a gruel diet and drugs such as Reglan and Propulsid to increase the movement of the esophagus.

Tumors of the spleen

The spleen is an organ in the blood system that disposes of old blood cells. In dogs, it also contains a large blood supply. Mastiffs are prone to tumors in the spleen, about half of which are malignant. If your Mastiff has a tumor in its spleen, the spleen will need to be removed.

Spinal cord problems

As Mastiffs age, they tend to develop degenerative disease in the bones of their vertebral column. This weakens the backbone and puts pressure on the intervertebral disks. Symptoms may include

- Lack of coordination. The dog walks as if it is drunk in the rear end.
- Dragging of the back feet (look for worn toenails)
- Stiff-legged walk
- Weakness in the back legs
- Muscle wasting in the hind end
- Discomfort when sitting

For mild cases, rest and anti-inflammatories can help your Mastiff. For more serious cases, short doses of steroids may be required. Surgery is also an option for the most severe cases.

Incompetent sphincters

Female Mastiffs commonly suffer from incompetent sphincters, leading them to urinate during their sleep. Phenylpropanolamine will help to control this. Note that phenylpropanolamine increases metabolism and heart rate and should not be used if your Mastiff has heart problems.

Prostate problems

Male Mastiffs who have not been neutered tend to develop prostate problems. The prostate becomes very large and can press on the urethra. This leads to painful urination and urine dribbling.

Prostate infections are also common in unneutered Mastiffs, and if untreated can lead to bone infections and swollen joints.

Arthritis

Arthritis is probably the most common problem for an aging Mastiff. Almost any Mastiff who lives long enough will have pain in its joints because of its size and weight. Treatment involves decreasing inflammation and trying to restore as much joint function as possible. Treatment options include

- Food additives that help repair damaged cartilage. These are usually marketed as nutraceuticals.
- Aspirin or aspirin-like drugs to reduce inflammation. Note that aspirin can cause ulcers, so stop giving your Mastiff aspirin immediately if it vomits.
- Exercise. Slow walks and swimming will help your Mastiff maintain muscle strength.

Mastiff Secrets

Chapter 12
RESOURCES AND FAQS

Resources

Want more information about Mastiffs? Check out these books and websites:

www.mastiffweb.com
www.mastiff.org
Mastiffs by Kim Thornton
Mastiff: A Comprehensive Guide to Owning and Caring for your Dog by Christina De Lima-Netto
The Complete Mastiff by Betty and David Baxter
The Mastiff: The Aristocratic Guardian by Dee Dee Andersson
The History and Management of the Mastiff by Elizabeth J. Baxter and Patricia B. Hoffman

Also, check to see whether your city has a Mastiff group. If one is not available. www.mastiffweb.com has a message board where you can meet and greet other Mastiff lovers.

FAQs

Where should I get a Mastiff?

If you want a puppy, the best choice is to buy one directly from a reputable breeder. How do you know if a breeder is reputable?

- Ask the local kennel club
- Visit dog shows
- Get a breeder referral list from the Mastiff Club of America (www.mastiff.org)

Once you think you have identified a reputable breeder, check the breeder's credentials, background, and contract. A reputable breeder will always take back or replace a puppy that is found to have a congenital defect. In addition, a breeder will help you choose a puppy with the right temperament to fit into your family.

What if I don't want a puppy?

Your best choice if you want an older Mastiff is to notify your local rescue group. Mastiffs sometime end up in rescue homes simply because their owners did not take into account their eventual size.

One issue with getting a Mastiff from a rescue group is that you don't know whether the Mastiff was properly trained and socialized as a puppy. Talk to the Mastiff's "foster family" if it had one to find out how it behaves in a home setting and how well-socialized the family judges it to be.

What about a pet shop?

It is never a good idea to buy a dog from a pet shop. Pet shops can give you no information about your dog's background or breeding, and the dog may have been exposed to untold diseases. In addition, a pet shop environment does not give a Mastiff puppy the early socialization it needs.

What about a backyard breeder?

It may be tempting to buy a Mastiff from your neighbor down the street who is breeding his own dog, especially if he is charging significantly less than the full-time breeder. However, you do not get the breeder's experience, careful selection of bloodlines to enhance the Mastiff breed, and extensive testing for congenital defects. In addition, the backyard breeder will probably not give you a contract to take back or replace a puppy that does have a congenital defect.

Should my Mastiff live indoors or out?

Mastiffs are truly happier indoors next to you. Mastiffs seem to have an instinctive need to be as close as possible to their human family, to the point that their emotional development and socialization can be stunted if they are deprived of that closeness. In fact, many breeders will refuse to sell a Mastiff unless the new owner guarantees that it will be kept as a house dog.

What kind of living quarters does a Mastiff require? Where do they sleep?

Mastiffs need a place of their own where they feel comfortable and secure. Wire crates are a practical solution, especially for a puppy being house-trained: they allow the Mastiff to see out and are harder to chew or destroy.

Another option is a pallet by your bed, whether a soft pad or a baby bed mattress covered with blankets. It is generally not a good idea to let a Mastiff sleep on the bed with you because of its eventual size. In addition, jumping off a bed is not good for the joints of a young Mastiff.

What other stuff do I need to buy for my Mastiff?

Your Mastiff will need toys, chew bones, collars and leashes, grooming equipment, and food and water dishes,

Toys

Toys need to be durable and able to withstand the Mastiff's tremendous strength. Always supervise your Mastiff with a new toy: if it rips the toy to shreds and starts swallowing the pieces, take the toy away.

Good toys for puppies include

- Children's stuffed animals and squeaky toys
- Plastic soda bottles with the cap and cap ring removed
- Knotted rope bones
- Large rope rings
- Soccer balls
- Basketballs

- Hard plastic or PVC balls
- Empty toilet paper and paper towel tubes
- Empty cardboard boxes
- Lawn mower tires

When your puppy becomes older than six months, take away the squeaky toys, plastic balls, and anything else that seems too small.

Chew bones

Good chew bones include

- Nylabones
- Kongs
- Vermont Chews (stuffed)
- Compressed rawhide bones
- Raw or sterilized beef bones

As your puppy grows, you will need to get larger and larger chew toys.

Collars and leashes

For a young puppy, an adjustable collar with a plastic snap is fine. After your puppy is about six months old, though, you will want to switch to a wide leather or nylon collar with a buckle. Be sure to get an ID tag made with your phone number and address on it just in case your Mastiff wanders away.

You will need different types of leashes for different purposes. For your own training at home, a six-foot nylon or leather leash works best, but you will want a shorter leash for going on walks. Just make sure all your leashes have strong snaps.

For formal training classes, you may need a metal "choke" chain. Ask your instructor what size to get and how to use it properly.

Grooming equipment

The basic equipment you will need includes a brush, nail clippers, and dog shampoo.

Food and water dishes

Stainless steel bowls are best because they are basically indestructible and are easy to wash and sterilize in the dishwasher.

You can start a puppy with smaller bowls, but by the time your Mastiff is full-grown, you will need the largest water bowl you can find and at least a five-quart bowl for food. It is also a good idea to elevate the food and water bowls. Elevated dishes can keep your Mastiff healthier because the animal won't have to splay its legs to get to the food and water. It can also help with digestion and possibly even reduce the chances of bloat. Eating while bent over forces dogs to gulp their food, and in the process, they swallow more air. This air can end up as foul-smelling gas a while later and may lead to bloat.

What are Mastiffs like in the house?

If you don't count the slobbering, Mastiffs are relatively clean. They don't shed a lot and they learn quickly to stay off furniture (unless you let them up there with you). They are also easy to housebreak.

How much slobber are we talking about?

Again, this depends on your individual dog. Most Mastiffs only drool when they

- Have just had a drink of water or eaten
- Are scared of something

It's a good idea to keep hand towels around to wipe your Mastiff's face before it can sling the slobber around the house or on you.

And how much do Mastiffs shed?

Mastiffs shed about twice a year. A daily brushing will prevent accumulation of hair around the house.

Do Mastiffs chew?

As a puppy, your Mastiff will probably chew. However, you can teach it proper behavior. You need to give your Mastiff puppy durable toys to chew on. If your puppy chews on anything except its own chew toys, take the forbidden item away and give the pup a chew toy. Especially remember to praise your puppy when it chews on his own toy.

Do Mastiffs bark much?

Puppies tend to bark more than adults because of their general excitement. Adults, however, rarely bark except when you arrive home or when they hear a doorbell or another sound they want you to investigate.

Do Mastiffs bite?

A Mastiff that is properly trained and socialized will typically not bite except as a last resort. Do not let puppies bite anyone or anything (except their littermates during playtime); this will teach them that biting is not allowed.

Do Mastiffs pass gas?

It depends on how the Mastiff reacts to the food it eats. Stick with good quality dog foods and minimize or eliminate table scraps. You may need to try a few different types of foods to find one that agrees with your Mastiff's digestive system.

Do Mastiffs roam?

Mastiffs tend to stay at home. However, because most cities have leash laws, it is best to keep your Mastiff on a leash or in a fenced yard when you are outside.

Do Mastiffs smell?

Mastiffs need occasional bathing with a good dog shampoo. If your Mastiff still smells despite regular baths, it may have a medical problem such as fungus in the ears or hypothyroidism.

If your Mastiff has bad breath, try brushing its teeth more regularly. If that doesn't help, have your vet check the teeth for dental problems.

Do Mastiffs snore?

Yes, Mastiffs do tend to be snorers. Snoring is genetic, so if you are really concerned about snoring, ask whether your Mastiff's mother and father are snorers.

How much does a Mastiff cost?

Puppy prices usually run $600-3000, depending on the animal's pedigree, show potential, geographic location, and breeder costs. A higher price does NOT necessarily mean a better dog, so investigate before you buy!

Does owning a Mastiff cost a lot?

A Mastiff costs more to maintain than smaller breeds because of its large size and weight. Everything simply costs more: larger crates, more food and toys, medicines that are prescribed based on weight, etc.

What does a Mastiff eat?

Mastiffs do best on a food that is

- In the medium range for protein (20-25%)
- In the mid range for fat (12-18%)
- Well-balanced for calcium and phosphorus
- High in iodine (3-5%)

Feeding your Mastiff puppy foods that are too high in protein, calories, and fat can make it grow too fast, possibly causing joint, ligament, and tendon problems.

How much does a Mastiff eat?

Despite their size, full-grown Mastiffs don't eat as much as you probably expect. Because they aren't very active, they eat about as much as a German shepherd.

Follow the recommendations on the dog food bag, adjusting the amount of food according to your Mastiff's body condition. Do not let your Mastiff get fat; fat dogs have many problems with bones and joints, heart, liver, kidney, etc. You should be able to feel your dog's ribs and see at least the last two ribs when the dog is moving.

How much does a Mastiff weigh?

Adult males generally weigh about 160 to 230 pounds, and females are normally between 120 and 170 pounds. According to the *Guinness Book of World Records*, the world's largest dog is a Mastiff named Zorba. At 343 pounds, Zorba stood 37 inches at the shoulder and was 8 foot 3 inches from the tip of his nose to the tip of his tail. Zorba set this record in November 1989, when he was eight years old.

Do Mastiffs need a lot of exercise?

Mastiffs need moderate exercise to reach their physical peak. Don't let a puppy overdo exercise, or it may develop joint problems. If you go for a long walk and your pup gets tired, be prepared to carry it home!

Do Mastiffs get along with children?

Mastiffs are gentle and protective, especially if they have been raised with children and are used to them. Be sure your children do not play roughly with a puppy; Mastiffs are a sensitive breed and can be permanently traumatized by rough handling.

Keep in mind that a Mastiff is large and powerful and can unintentionally injure a child or even an infirm adult, especially if it gets excited and begins wagging its tail exuberantly. If you have young children, you might consider waiting until they are older and stronger before introducing a Mastiff into your family.

Do Mastiffs get along with other dogs?

Mastiffs are typically friendly toward other dogs unless they were not properly socialized as puppies. However, if your Mastiff tends to have a dominant personality, it is best not to place it in a household with another dominant dog, especially of the same sex.

If your Mastiff is aggressive, try —

- Additional training
- Having your vet check for physical problems such as hypothyroidism
- Spaying or neutering your dog
- Switching to a food that is lower in protein

Do Mastiffs get along with other animals?

Again, early socialization and exposure is key here. A Mastiff that was never exposed to cats, hamsters, farm animals, etc. when young may treat them as prey. If your Mastiff didn't receive this socialization, you will need to do additional training.

Do Mastiffs get along with strangers?

A properly socialized Mastiff should stand beside you politely when a stranger is around. It may possibly be aloof until it sees your positive reaction to someone, after which it will become friendlier.

Do Mastiffs make good guard dogs?

Mastiffs are naturally protective of their families and don't need additional guard dog training. If they feel a person is threatening, they will get between their family and the perceived threat. A Mastiff typically won't attack, but just act as a large, protective barrier.

If someone breaks into your house, your Mastiff will probably corner the intruder until a family member gets home to deal with the situation. It may snarl, bark or even snap at the intruder, but usually will not attack unless provoked.

How much training does a Mastiff need?

Because they grow so large, every Mastiff should have basic obedience training. They need to learn the following commands:

- Sit
- Down
- Stay
- Come

They also need to be properly socialized and to learn to walk on a leash. Socialization is an extremely important part of a puppy's training. An unsocialized Mastiff can become either fearful or aggressive.

Most Mastiffs are easy to train because they are so eager to please. They are generally easier to train when they are young.

A Mastiff does not need protection training. Even the gentlest Mastiff will protect its family if it is socialized and bonded to them.

To find obedience and socialization classes, ask your local Kennel Clubs and veterinarians. If you cannot find a class, take your puppy out often to places where it can meet people and other dogs in a friendly atmosphere.

Do Mastiffs make good obedience dogs?

Mastiffs are eager to please, which generally makes them good candidates for the Obedience ring. However, temperament varies from dog to dog, so you will need to evaluate whether your dog has the right temperament.

Do Mastiffs make good therapy dogs?

Mastiffs can make excellent therapy dogs, as long as they have been well-socialized and are calm and gentle. If you think your Mastiff might be a good candidate as a therapy dog, you will need to have it certified for therapy work through an organization such as Therapy Dog International. As part of the certification, the dog will be introduced to items such as wheelchairs and walkers, to see how it responds.

What colors are Mastiffs?

Mastiffs come in apricot, brindle, and various shades of fawn. They may have some white on the chest.

How long does a Mastiff live?

The average Mastiff lives for six to 10 years.

What health problems do Mastiffs tend to have?

Mastiffs are prone to the following genetic or acquired health problems:

- Joint problems such as hip and elbow dysplasia and arthritis
- Cataracts, retinal detachment, glaucoma, progressive retinal atrophy (PRA), and other eye problems that can cause blindness
- Hypothyroidism
- Demodectic mange
- Myasthenia gravis
- Cherry eye, dry eye, and retinal folds.
- Skin allergies
- Heart murmurs
- Kidney and bladder infections
- Ear infections
- Bloat

What kind of a temperament does a Mastiff have?

Mastiffs are called gentle giants because of their generally benign and benevolent character. However, like people, Mastiffs are highly individual: some are placid and easy-going while others are higher energy. It also depends at least somewhat on how well the Mastiff was socialized while young.

How much grooming does a Mastiff need?

You should brush your Mastiff and check its ears daily. The toenails need to be clipped weekly, and it needs a bath around once a month or whenever it starts to smell too "doggy."

Are there any famous book and movie Mastiffs?

The movies *The Sandlot* and *Sandlot 2* both feature Mastiffs, as do *The Secret Garden* and *Meet Wally Sparks*. The most famous book Mastiff is Mudge of the *Henry and Mudge* children's book series.

What's the difference between a Mastiff and a Bullmastiff?

The Mastiff is an ancient breed that can be traced back more than 2,000 years. The Bullmastiff is a more recent breed developed from crossing the Mastiff with the bulldog. The most noticeable differences between the two breeds are temperament, head shape, and overall size. Bullmastiffs have more energy and are more stubborn than Mastiffs. Their foreheads are flatter and their muzzles shorter. They are also shorter, more compact, and more muscular. They weigh far less than Mastiffs: males are 110 to 130 pounds and females are 100 to 120 pounds.

Made in the USA
Lexington, KY
18 September 2010